CONCILIUM
Theology in the Age of Renewal

CONCILIUM

Theology in the Age of Renewal

EDITORIAL DIRECTORS: Edward Schillebeeckx (Dogma) · Herman Schmidt (Liturgy) · Alois Müller (Pastoral) · Hans Küng (Ecumenism) · Franz Böckle (Moral Theology) · Johannes B. Metz (Church and World) · Roger Aubert (Church History) · ✠Néophytos Edelby and Teodoro Jiménez Urresti (Canon Law) · Christian Duquoc (Spirituality) · Pierre Benoit and Roland Murphy (Scripture)

CONSULTING EDITORS: Marie-Dominique Chenu · ✠Carlo Colombo · Yves Congar · Andrew Greeley · Jorge Mejía · Karl Rahner · Roberto Tucci

EXECUTIVE SECRETARY: Jan Micklinghoff, Arksteestraat 3-5, Nijmegen, The Netherlands

Volume 53: Pastoral Theology

EDITORIAL BOARD: Editor: Alois Müller · Assistant Editors: Karl Lehmann · Nobert Greinacher · Associate Editors: Willem Bekkum · Martin Ekwa · Rafael Espin Lastra · Adolf Exeler · Henri-Marie Féret · Casiano Floristán · Domenico Grasso · Alfonso Gregory · Frans Haarsma · Adrian Hastings · Johannes Hofinger · Francois Houtart · Jan Kerkhofs · James Killgallon · Ferdinand Klostermann · Jean Le Du · Francois Lepargneur · Angelo Macchi · Józef Majka · Luis Maldonado · Barthélemy Nyom · Juan Ochagavía · Gustavo Pérez Ramírez · Emile Pin · Karl Rahner · José Rodriguez Medina · Victor Schurr · Heinz Schuster · Gerard Sloyan · Anthony Spencer · Theodore Steeman · Rolf Zerfass

CATECHETICS
FOR THE FUTURE

Edited by
Alois Müller

Herder and Herder

1970
HERDER AND HERDER
232 Madison Avenue, New York 10016

Cum approbatione Ecclesiastica

Library of Congress Catalog Card Number: 76-110787
Copyright © 1970 by Herder and Herder, Inc., and Stichting Concilium. All rights reserved. Nothing contained in this publication shall be reproduced and/or made public by means of print, photographic print, microfilm, or in any other manner without the previous consent of the Stichting Concilium and the publishers.

Printed in the United States

CONTENTS

Editorial   7

PART I

ARTICLES

Communicating the Faith in Present-day Society   13
RAMÓN ECHARREN

A Modern Approach to Catechesis in the Church as a
Whole   22
JOSEPH COLOMB

Education and Catechetics   34
ADOLF EXELER

Beyond the Bible in Religious Education   43
KARL ERNST NIPKOW

Language Problems and Catechetics   56
JEAN LE DU

PART II

STUDIES

A Catechesis adapted to the Present Age and the
Liturgical Initiation of Children   69
CHRISTIANE BRUSSELMANS

New Directions in Catechetics in the Missions   77
SYLVESTER WEVITAVIDANELAGE

Language in the Dutch Catechism   84
TJEU VAN DEN BERK, F.S.C.

PART III

BULLETIN

What are the Main Requirements for a New Catechism?   93
WILLEM BLESS, S.J.

Guiding Principles for Catechesis among the Yoruba
of Nigeria   98
BERNARD MANGEMATIN, W.F.

Some Guidelines for a New American Catechism   103
JOSEPH B. COLLINS

The New Polish Catechism   109
FRANCISZEK BLACHNICKI

The Development of the Bible Lesson in German
Catechetics   116
WOLFGANG LANGER

Problems of Bible Instruction in American Catechetical
Literature   128
IRIS V. CULLY

"Renewed" Catechisms in South America   140
ONÉSIMO O'GORMAN, F.M.S.

Reflections on the Isolotto Catechism   152
LUIGI DELLA TORRE

Editorial

THIS ISSUE is devoted to a study of the function of catechetics, or religious education. The subject will be seen and treated from the viewpoint of its specific function within the Church's pastoral effort as a whole, and we shall want to see to what extent it meets the requirements of the times. Our primary object is to form a clearer picture of the structure catechetical praxis should have today. For obvious reasons, an international journal like *Concilium* cannot cater for the urgent needs of every local situation; we cannot, for instance, produce ready-to-use lesson plans. There are other journals and media that do this more appropriately. What we have attempted, by commissioning contributions from a wide area, is to identify the fundamental questions that face contemporary catechetics, and in this process to highlight a few of its most important practical tasks.

A selection of these "imperatives for a catechetics for the future" is provided in the articles. The reader will observe the astonishing extent to which the authors agree on major emphases in spite of other differences that can be observed in their outlook. The fundamental questions facing catechetics today become even more acute in a context of a proclamation of faith that does justice to the human situation, for such a proclamation is determined not only by theological factors, but also by educational theory, psychology, sociology, cultural anthropology, linguistics, and so on. It is the first article's modest task, by way of introduction, to remind readers of what this implies for catechetical theory and practice.

7

Orientation in the matter of catechetical practice, and the connection between catechetics as science and its concrete application, is furnished through detailed Bulletins and a questionnaire. There are also detailed reports from the German and American viewpoints on the problems connected with the Bible lesson. An annotated bibliography provides some valuable information about the perhaps little known catechetical renewal in Latin America. The Isolotto Catechism is subjected to close study (an analysis of the problems that beset the Isolotto community and its priests does not come within the scope of this issue). The questionnaire is self-explanatory (but see special Introduction).

Questions of method (which, correctly understood, are inseparable from the main object of catechesis) are also considered. On matters of particular importance contributors have been at pains to comment on the comparable situation obtaining in the field of non-Catholic catechetics (cf. Wolfgang Langer's article). We are particularly grateful for the collaboration of two non-Catholic colleagues, K. E. Nipkow and I. V. Cully.

In order not to make the issue as a whole unduly long, one major article had to be dropped from the original plan. It was to have treated of the Christian faith's fundamental need for catechesis, and would have gone into the following questions: Why is it natural to *Christian* faith (different in this respect from other religions) to require catechesis? What is the object of catechesis when it is not merely the abstract communication of knowledge, or the reproduction of factual data? What are we to make of the fact that in many respects it is of the essence of Christian faith that it be "learned"? Mentioning this article here might help to remove misunderstandings concerning the "imperatives for a catechetics for the future" presented in this issue, and at the same time help to justify the composition of the issue as a whole.

We are unable, of course, to treat every important theme, let alone every "decisive" one. Passing references only could be made to the connection between liturgy and catechetics, sacramental catechetics, the relationship between adult catechetics and the provision of adult theological education, and to many other problems. It has been noticeable that the treatment of these and other themes from the field of catechetics required intensive co-operation among the various theological disciplines (which in the case of *Concilium* has meant drawing upon the resources of other sections of the journal).

Perhaps the issue as a whole has benefited from the pressures of space in that the result has been a hopefully useful concentration on particular problems. Readers should not be alarmed by the predominance of questions of principle and method, for sometimes it is not so much a question of "content" alone—vital though this is—as of the yardstick by which the whole is to be seen and understood. Perhaps it is this "fresh glance" of which we are most in need. As science, catechetics cannot provide all the answers, but there is no reason why it should not help to prepare the way.

ALOIS MÜLLER
KARL LEHMANN
NORBERT GREINACHER

PART I
ARTICLES

Ramón Echarren

Communicating the Faith in Present-day Society

I. Human Experience and the Truths of Faith

ALL religious instruction proclaims the Word of God and therefore aims to promote and nourish the life of faith.

But the richness and complexity of faith can never be adequately expressed as the knowledge with which theological analysis may identify it in its most formal aspect; it cannot be reduced to a simple, straightforward possession of revealed truths. Faith involves the whole man, for it is a man's free and total response to the Word of God.[1]

Therefore the purpose of religious instruction is to introduce all men and the "whole man" to the Word of God seeking to take root in them. This purpose is achieved when a personal commitment accompanies the assent of faith.

Revelation is not something dropped out of the sky to communicate transcendental mysteries to mankind, externally and from on high. God speaks to man from within the world and from within human experience.[2]

Because he can refer to the events and circumstances of his human condition, man is able to grasp that the truth revealed by God is not alien, but something which intimately affects his life. The Christian message cannot be absorbed by someone who has

---

[1] J. Mouroux, *Je Crois en toi* (Du Cerf), Chapter III, pp. 45 ff.
[2] Cf. H. Urs von Balthasar, *Parole de Dieu et Liturgie* (Du Cerf), p. 86.

not discovered its "realistic" understanding of God as present and active in the midst of human existence.[3]

Like a form of language, human experiences constitute the framework within which, throughout his life, a believer constantly reformulates his image of God.[4] He asks questions within the same framework that dispose him to see the Bible as the answer to his particular queries (Karl Barth).

To posit this connection between human experience and the truths of faith or faith itself is not to imply that the truth alters. But reality itself and one's vision of reality do alter.[5] To hold that absolute truth has appeared once and for all, regardless of any linguistic medium and of any re-presentation springing from human experience, is to be unaware of the structure of language and implicitly to deny God's intention to speak to man in man's own language, which is the only one man understands. To limit absolute truth with past ways of representing it is retrogressive and can arrest the dynamism of the religious man or the religious element in man.

It is only possible to accept a truth of faith and to embody it in a deep personal outlook if one makes sense of it from within the same cultural system of reference as that which normally governs one's thinking.

In part, the success of an attempt to convey the truths of faith will depend as much on the type of culture affecting their recipient as on that influencing their mediator. Hence one must know the person who is to receive the message, if one is to choose an appropriate linguistic vehicle.[6]

Every sender of a message has to cast his ideas in the vocabulary, symbols and images of his culture, and the recipient has to interpret them according to those of his own culture. The interaction between culture and the content of knowledge does not

---

[3] Cf. J. Le Du, "Catéchèse, précatéchèse", in *Catéchèse*, No. 21, October 1965.

[4] J. Le Du, "Catéchèse et Anthropologie", in *Catéchèse*, No. 24, July 1966.

[5] Cf. E. Schillebeeckx, *Révélation et Théologie* (C.E.P., Brussels), pp. 224 and 225.

[6] J. Le Du, "Catéchèse et Anthropologie", in *Catéchèse*, No. 24, July 1966.

only occur "on the level of" mental and verbal forms, but—in some way—affects the very essence of what is known.[7]

Therefore we have to get to know the man of today; discover the psychological and social mechanisms which affect his acceptance of the message; and understand the cultural world which defines and conditions him.

The problem is not just one of a theological notion of Church and world. Such an approach is urgently needed; but it is not enough in itself.

The problem needs to be looked at from another angle. We have to discover the man of today while conscious that we, the discoverers, are men of today ourselves. We have to find him from within. As Christians we must not be men of the past—condescending, paternalistic observers of the spectacle of our fellow men living and loving, working, enjoying themselves, suffering and dying. Man as he really is is right next to us, "flung into existence". We must carefully avoid replacing man as he actually speaks, laughs, sorrows and toils, with a mere re-fashioned image from the past; we shall understand him better only if we immerse ourselves in the reality of what it means to be a human being.[8]

II. PROFOUND CHANGE IN MODERN SOCIETY

Mankind today is changing profoundly. Physical data, the organization of society, social relations, systems of communication and ways of thinking are altering radically. Humanity has entered an era in which change has become the norm, and adaptation to change a fundamental value. Our highly socialized society has given man a new vision of his position in the world; of what his relations with other men are, could and should be; of the value of solidarity; of the requirements of a morality in which

[7] Cf. J. Laloux, *Manual de iniciación a la Sociología Religiosa* (Nova Terra, 1968), pp. 158–60.

[8] Cf. F. Houtart, *La Iglesia y el mundo* (Nova Terra, 1965); J. Labbens, *L'Eglise et les centres urbains* (Spes, 1958); J. Laloux, *Manual de iniciación a la Sociología Religiosa* (Nova Terra, 1968); J. Delcourt, "La transmission du Message Chrétien à la lumière de la Sociologie de la communication", in *Les Dossiers*, No. 12, February 1965; G. Rotureau, *Conscience religieuse et mentalité technique* (Desclée, 1962).

"other people" must in some way be taken into account; and of the need to find fulfilment through co-operative effort, i.e., through teamwork. This greater dependence of men upon each other effects a new relationship between the individual and society in which numerous counter-balancing factors play an important part: a democratic outlook; the supreme value attached to the dignity of the person; the desire for emancipation from every form of authoritarianism, formal or informal; the rejection of tradition as a limitation on the autonomy of one's own decisions; the insistence on the total respect of personal privacy; the right of the individual to speech, thought and opinion that are free in the sense of being without all coercion, social pressure, and so on.

In addition, the gradual shortening of distances—as a result of technological progress in all the means of communication—is helping to create a real global unity in the emergence of a universal collective consciousness or will to guide mankind, however much it costs, towards a more human social order for all men.

The same facts have led men to take stock of forms of life other than their own, and of other ways of thinking and behaving. Numerous points of difference are dissolved in this way, while the range of diversity increases. All this leads of necessity to a pluralist system, to the indispensable peaceful coexistence of differing points of view in economics, politics, social life and religion. The need for coexistence and the need for openness to the world are equally conducive to an ecumenical outlook.

The development of the positive sciences and of their technical application is one of the fundamental marks of our time.[9] The significance for humanity which we allow science nowadays stems from the fact that scientific awareness is, as it were, the homage paid by the human spirit to the truth which is beyond us, yet nourishes our freedom and makes claims upon our responsibility. Humble submission to the facts and to the rigorous requirements of scientific method; total freedom in investigation, without prejudice or any *"a priori"*; the sense that one is responsible before the whole of mankind for the precious and in some way sacred value of the disinterested service of truth; the patience and the

---

[9] Cf. A. Dondeyne, *La foi écoute le monde* (Editions Universitaires, Paris, 1964).

will-power not to give up investigating in spite of failures and successes: these are the virtues which convert scientific awareness into a supreme ethical value.[10] Technology sharpens man's sense of the efficacy of reason, precision and objectivity. "Truth", "authenticity" and "sincerity" are sought after as means of getting rid of all a-scientific "obscurantism", "covering up" and falsity separating man from "the real". Modern man strips his work of all artificial ornamentation in order to preserve the truth of the original raw materials and to endow the purely "functional" aspects of form and volume with beauty.

With his keen sense of the perfectibility through technology of matter both living and inert, modern man begins to feel that human history is also perfectible. Refusing to accept a fatalistic view of his destiny, he looks forward to forging his own personal future and to helping to make a collective destiny for mankind. Modern man seeks a natural explanation for everything. Scientific progress has convinced him that all natural phenomena—including the biological life of man—are subject to identical laws and should primarily be explained in terms of them. There should, therefore, be no cause for surprise at the present desacralization of the world.[11]

The attraction of temporal realities perfected through technology, the awakening of a progressive and democratic outlook, ideological and institutional pluralism, and the value of sincerity have given rise to a real secularization or desacralization, that is, to a world in which the temporal is conceived as a value in itself and as an autonomous reality.

Twentieth-century man lives in a heterogeneous environment and within complex social structures. The division of labour, the new types of human relations multiplying with the increasing number of facilities and forms of association made use of by man, geographical mobility brought about by modern means of transport and communication—all these cut him off more and more from his fellow men. The formation required of him if he is to fit into this complex tends to ensure that his period of instruction

[10] Cf. A. Dondeyne, op. cit.
[11] A. Dondeyne, op. cit.

lasts not just for a part of his life, but becomes what Armand[12] calls a "system of permanent education".[13]

In society today there is a growing tendency to separate the basic elements of the main cultural and value systems, that is, the elements corresponding to religion, philosophy and science. There is also a spread of literacy and of secular education. Because of specialization it has a more complex, intellectual framework.[14]

In this society (increasingly mobile[15] geographically, socially and socio-culturally), the increase in human loneliness is a real threat. Human relations are becoming specialized and functional.

There are two contradictory forces at work today in the sphere of human relations: one is conducive to anonymity and isolation; the other leads to the recognition or increasing awareness of human loneliness. The former tends towards a reduction in the number of relationships and to an increasing concentration on their intensity and intimacy. The latter results in the attempt to find in small groups the community lacking in ordinary life.

In spite of all this, the private life of the individual acquires more and more importance, not in the sense that man acts in private, that is, individually, but in the sense that ultimately these acts are only fully known by the individual himself. This preponderance of the private side of life contributes most towards the anonymity in which modern man lives today.

Another characteristic of our society is what we might call the predominance of the image. As a result of the spread of television, cinema and advertising media, man today really leads a life based on visual information. This form of existence imposes a new style on human relations, on family life, on every type of living together, on language, and so on. Man finds himself at the mercy of whatever the images suggest to him. At the same time he has made himself sensitive to current affairs to the exclusion of practically everything else. His interest lies always in

[12] L. Armand and M. Dorancourt, *Plaidoyer pour l'avenir* (Calmann-Levy, Paris, 1961), p. 168.

[13] F. Houtart, *op. cit.*, p. 68.

[14] E. Shils, "Political Development in New States", in *Comparative Studies in History and Society*, July 1960; K. Mannheim, *Man and Society in an Age of Reconstruction* (Routledge and Kegan Paul, London, 1940).

[15] Cf. K. W. Deutsch, "Social Mobilization and Political Development", in *American Political Science Review*, No. 55, September 1961.

movement and he feels less and less amenable to what has gone before. As advertising and the mass media concern themselves continually with news it is not easy for contemporary man to find the opportunity to reflect and to become deeply involved in the facts they communicate to him.[16]

III. The Task of Catechetics

If it is difficult to grasp what it means to be a human being to-day, it is even more difficult to establish the necessary link between human experience and the truths of faith.

Faith should first and foremost create a new man; it should give a supernatural meaning to the whole of his activity by stimulating and directing it.[17]

For faith to do this we must have anthropologically up-to-date linguistic formulae for the truths of faith.

All religious instruction should be an encounter and a challenge. It should take human experience for what it truly is and adopt its most positive values, but force man to question himself and to seek his highest meaning in a way that will allow him to be open to a true conversion.

A catechetics for today should not simply make use of modern means of expression but should also take the inductive path which will lead men from the visible to the invisible, from the aspirations contained in the myths of our time and from their temporal projection, to the aspirations which find their fulfilment in revelation.

Our methods of religious instruction have adopted linguistic formulae taken from almost exclusively traditional frameworks. This explains the difficulty there is in relating them to human experience today.

Socialization, planetization; pluralism, ecumenism; positivism, pragmatism and technology; progress, effectiveness, reason; objectivity, activism; desacralization, democracy; functionalism, specialization, permanent apprenticeship; the defence of privacy

[16] Cf. A. Merland, "Valeur anthropologique de l'imaginaire", in *Catéchèse*, No. 18, January 1965.

[17] John XXIII, "Princeps Pastorum", *Documentations Catholiques* (1959), col. 1, 548.

and the search for personal relationships: all these constitute a frame of reference within which it becomes extremely difficult to insert a Christian message expressed in cultural terms which highlight formulae obviously opposed to the characteristic concerns of men today.

Nevertheless the task is not only feasible but relatively simple. It is ultimately a question of really living in the contemporary world.

As Laloux points out,[18] sociological and anthropological studies indicate that the relation between knowledge and culture is not just a question of words and images as verbal forms, but above all a question of values, of a way of looking at things, of special meanings, of legitimizations; it is closely bound up with the degree of scientific knowledge of objective realities and with the types of reasoning in current use in the social environment. In other words, it is a question of "mental forms".

To pass a message from one culture to another it is necessary not just to decode and rephrase the message via a linguistic translation but also to "deculturalize" it (as regards values, concepts and special meanings) by taking it out of one socio-cultural context and placing it in a new one. Only in this way can one be certain of preserving a true knowledge, acceptance and assimilation of the message within the new culture. This operation requires rather more than a simple cultural translation of the message. In a sense it also affects the content of the message itself, in that it involves a new process of selection which includes eliminating certain aspects and substituting others so that what is finally transmitted, understood and assimilated is identical with the original message.

To realize all this it is only necessary to study the history of the Church. Think, for example, of the development of theological formulae, of the Church's identity, of the Mystical Body of Christ or of the varying importance attached to these in the life of the people of God in the course of its history.[19]

To ask oneself how the Christian message formulated in a culture different from our own is currently perceived and

[18] *Op. cit.*, pp. 158-9.
[19] Cf. J. Le Du, "Catéchèse et Anthropologie", in *Catéchèse*, No. 24, July 1966.

absorbed, and to adapt its form (and even, to some extent, its content) so that the same message is taken in, is very, very important for a right approach to catechetics.

The fundamental truths of the faith have now been expressed in so many ways that it is difficult to grasp its immense riches. That in no way implies, however, that the highly socialized, technical, rationalized, planetary and personalized character of our society has nothing to offer in the way of categories in which we can better express the true face of Christ for contemporary man. But in any event these new re-presentations must be the product of what without doubt has prepared them: the "memory" of the Church.[20]

All religious instruction requires an underlying anthropology which will permit us to get closer to supernatural realities without falling into empty wordiness. The big task of contemporary catechetics is to work out a presentation of the faith which will bring us closer to God and closer to the historical reality of human life.

[20] Cf. J. Le Du, *loc. cit.*

Translated by Jonathan Cavanagh

Joseph Colomb

A Modern Approach to Catechesis in the Church as a Whole

A FULL treatment of the subject of this article would require many pages; two points only can be emphasized here: (1) At the present time in the Church primary importance should be given to the catechesis of adults; and (2) this catechesis must provide a formation in certain attitudes of faith required by modern times.

In many countries, certainly in those of the French and English-speaking worlds, the emphasis in the last few decades has been placed on the catechesis of children; then, with the raising of the school-leaving age and the appearance of adolescents as a "social class" it became increasingly necessary to catechize them also. At the present time, the conviction is gaining ground that (without of course neglecting children and adolescents) catechesis should be concerned still more with adults.

I. REASONS FOR THE PRIMARY IMPORTANCE OF ADULT CATECHESIS

It is true, of course, that the child cannot understand problems of faith encountered by the adolescents, nor the latter the problems of faith of the adult, the middle-aged or the aged. To claim that one can provide the child or the adolescent with all that he will need in this respect during his whole life is obviously contrary to all the most elementary principles of psychology and sociology. It is contrary especially to the outlook prevailing in a period of development like the present when people no longer save their money, but buy as and when they need something (and know the right place at which to buy it) and are everywhere subject to the reorganization and re-styling of life. I shall return to this last remark.

Because the adult is man at the stage of full development, he is capable of "understanding" in a balanced and spiritual way the different aspects of the message of Christ. Of necessity it is he who furnishes in the world complete witness to the full faith of the Church; he it is who can confront the faith with the findings of human thought and science. A church in which the adults, especially, are deprived of religious instruction cannot be a humanly adult church.

In addition, the adult is quite certainly the principal educator of children and adolescents, even though the latter also educate each other. The adult will be able to perform his function as a Christian educator of children and adolescents only if he has received the proper instruction and his faith is adult, if he is capable of understanding Christ's answer to the spiritual needs of youth. It must also be pointed out here that the religious education of children and adolescents is always compromised when they see that adults have none themselves, that catechesis is something for children and that faith seems unable to confront the adult mind and throw light on the various human problems encountered by the adult.

The need for adult catechesis is all the more important now that we are at a turning-point in the life of the Church in which the increase in the status of the laity is the chief factor. Now these two problems—the increase in status of the laity and adult catechesis—are closely related. Religious teaching such as is given until the age of twelve (in a Christian environment) is suitable to train those who *practise* their religion; instruction of adolescents, if it makes the faith a personal matter, can produce convinced and active Christians; but if a man is actually to assume the responsibility of the kingdom of God—and this can only be done by an adult—he must have been able to discover the "social" responsibilities of the faith and the harsh world in which it must be spread abroad. On the other hand, in the usual state of ignorance of the laity, it is impossible for them to play an active part and take on the responsibilities required of them, and especially those demanded by the changes to be introduced into the life of the Church.

Perhaps we are too apt to think that people's refusal to commit themselves, or their passive attitude, springs primarily from a lack of generosity. We forget that it is impossible to act and undertake something if the mind is not the predominant factor in the action, if a man does not possess clear and deep convictions enabling him to know where he is going and to understand the meaning of the difficulties that he faces. I should not like to think that a fuller knowledge of the Christian mystery among the laity should cause some people to fear that it would make the government of the Christian community a more difficult task and deprive the clergy of their complete freedom in the apostolic ministry. On the contrary, I feel that I have observed among many parish priests a feeling of powerlessness and of the practical impossibility of giving their adult laity the catechesis that they expect and on occasion demand. If it is indeed true that new problems can be caused by the increased status of the laity, it is quite certain that there can be no question of avoiding them, and that a genuine adult catechesis is one of the best means of providing a positive solution for them. We should remember in this connection that Vatican II, in the decree on the apostolate of the laity, n. 29 and n. 32, has already shown the path to be followed and the principles for the formation of the laity for their own form of apostolate.

II. REQUIREMENTS OF THE DIFFERENT AGE GROUPS

The progress achieved in the catechesis of children and adolescents implies that a fairly long investigation has been carried out into their secular and religious psychology and the influences affecting them. It seems obvious that the same will hold good in the case of adults. It may seem that by the time a man reaches adulthood he is in a balanced and tranquil state. Actually he continues to develop, he passes through new crises, perhaps less apparent but just as profound as those of youth: crises of action, of limitations, of retirement. Now these situations are also those of faith. For faith must continue to be instructed and defended, and to develop in relation to very clear needs; catechesis, which always aims at the education of faith, must therefore be aware of the problems that it has to meet, the dangers that it must enable people to overcome, and so on. A few words must be said here about the twenty-five to forty-five or fifty age group, and also the aged.[1]

Roughly speaking, it can be said that the adult becomes responsible for this world; in him the world and the society of men is made real, is re-created and spiritualized. This responsibility is to be seen in the struggle between the ideal and reality; it is accomplished with others in various social relationships; it is dialogue, collaboration and offering. The adult forms his personality in the process of constructing his home and his professional and cultural life. His faith is one of action. But as a consequence he is in danger of losing himself in this activity, of alienating himself in the lack of reflection and perspective, of becoming torn between the multiplicity of his tasks, of being restricted within the confines of this activity and of becoming set in his ways. His faith will have to be educated so that it can be a creative source, and also an inspiration to struggle, social action, spiritual life, self-mastery based on the love of God. The religious instruction will reflect the adult's real needs.

The same can be said of the aged. To talk of instructing the aged in their faith may well astonish many Catholics and even priests. The aged, in a world of obvious efficiency, are still sorely neglected, even in the Church, and it is difficult to see what their special function is. Yet, in the face of Christian death, which is a passing over and development, this role is an important one. The old person can settle down to the spiritual experience of the end of his days, which is the very opposite of despair; his very nature turns him towards spiritual passivity in the hands of God, and self-abandonment is his profound attitude of soul together with patience, kindness, the fruit of experience, charity which renders small service to others, the spirit of detachment, trust in God and time for prayer. Old men or women can be witnesses in the Church to hope and the risen life. Their religious instruction, therefore, will have to be one of hope, and Christian death, of trusting abandon to God. In this it will be in harmony with their real situation, their needs and their role in the Church.

[1] This is developed further in my *Le Service de l'Evangile*, II (Desclée St Jean, Tournai, 1968), pp. 415-53.

III. Methods and Means of Adult Catechesis

It must be said in the first place that adult catechesis is still in its infancy and that we must learn from the various attempts and experiments. Notice, too, that many different means can and must co-operate in this adult catechesis. Books, reviews, illustrated periodicals can exert a great influence. In this context one naturally thinks of the Dutch Catechism or the series *Fêtes et Saisons* in France (of which a few numbers were translated into English in the U.S.A.). For older people, a review (*Notre temps*) has been started. Radio and television are already making their contribution to this catechesis through interviews, televised sermons and so on, and probably their role will increase in importance.

On the other hand, as regards more methodical catechesis, several different levels must be distinguished: a number of religious conferences take place, biblical and theological lectures are already being given, at a certain cultural level and aimed directly more at dealing with objective problems than with educating the attitude of faith. In addition, even for the laity, there can be catechesis of a more scientific kind that is much nearer technical theology. Some theological faculties give a degree in religious instruction; as a matter of fact, at the present time the Church has great need of laymen capable of teaching religion competently.

But I am thinking here more particularly of a continuous or permanent catechesis addressed to Christians as a whole, and aimed at education of faith in the sense explained above; here there will be "re-organization" from time to time determined by the very development of life and human situations, by the crises and new developments of faith. A catechesis of this kind, which can always be completed by instruction at a higher theological level, would be in direct succession to the catechesis of children and adolescents; it would be addressed to all.

Notice in this connection that the Sunday sermon has often performed the function of such a catechesis. Preaching has often been in sermon or catechetical form precisely because there was no other possibility of adult catechesis. But if preaching really takes the form of a homily, intended principally to edify and to knit the congregation together for the sacrificial action, another form of catechesis is necessary, one that is more explanatory in approach and nearer, too, to daily life, which will also be the best preparation for the liturgical action.

It is clear, therefore, that a special kind of catechesis is required. If the "active method" is already usual with children, *a fortiori* it should be brought into use with adults who realize their own problems and difficulties. The dialogue between catechized and catechist should find a place before, during and after catechesis; discussion in groups will probably be usual; the problems raised by day-to-day activities will never, of course, be far away and there will always be concern to see that this consideration of them is reflected in daily life. On many points where the conditions of Christian daily life "in the world" are concerned the Christians themselves, that is the "catechized", will have to provide the answer in the light of the word of God; having listened to it the priest will often find it necessary, no doubt, to state it more clearly and in proper terms. Trained members of the laity are not excluded from presiding over catechesis of this kind, far from it. In this way we shall avoid the paradox of children's catechism classes in which the ignorant pupils answer questions from the well-informed master.

A number of matters are raised by catechesis of this kind. For example, when should it take place? In this case, especially, experience will reveal the various possibilities. The following can be put forward as a suggestion: traditionally Lent is a time of enlightenment for the whole Church for faith or a more enlightened faith. Is it not suitable as a time for catechesis? In this case meetings would be held once or twice a week for the different age groups. It may well be thought that the conditions of modern life will lead to these meetings being held from Advent to Easter. But to solve the practical difficulties one thing is particularly necessary, and that is the profound conviction of the need for catechesis on a permanent basis. Failing this conviction, unsurmountable difficulties will arise at every turn.

IV. SPIRITUAL OUTLOOK OF CATECHESIS AT THE PRESENT TIME

I should like now to consider not so much the various aspects of the message which the Church's catechesis must emphasize at the present day, as the spirit in which it is to be imparted. Then, too, there are the attitudes of faith that it must strive to encourage, the states of mind with which it is confronted that often condition it to some extent. Experience has shown the gaps frequently to be found nowadays in the faith of many Christians, even those who practise; our catechesis should be aimed at filling these gaps.

1. *Prudence and Frankness*

It must not be forgotten that most Christians of mature age are currently having to effect a veritable revolution in their faith. They have been trained according to the principles of a Christian way of life which has given them a habit of mind and an understanding of the Church, the sacraments, the apostolate and the truths of religion in general which is rather different from what is required in our present "diaspora" situation, and expressed in the documents of Vatican II.[2] That is why at this time and for some years to come adult catechesis will need to observe a certain prudence and discretion. And yet it must be frank, for many feel keenly that their faith is childish, out of date, humanly inferior to that of their children; at the present time "scandalizing of the weak" is not to be feared so much provided care is taken to build up rather than to destroy. In addition, it must be shown that some new way of presenting the message represents progress in faith.

2. *Coherence, Unity and Centres of Gravity*

In a certain sense, Christian layfolk possess knowledge of many matters (and that is still truer since newspapers and radio and television have come into common use) but what they lack is coherence, unity and depth in these matters.[3] It is not so much a question of increasing the range of their knowledge, but rather of being concerned to show forth the simplicity and unity in Christ

[2] I would refer the reader once again to *Le Service de l'Evangile*, where I develop the points made here; see especially II, pp. 536–9, 549–54, 605, 610. Many other points could be made in this article if space allowed, and are to be found in the work already mentioned.

[3] G. Duperray, "Un essai de catéchèse d'adultes", in *Catéchèse* (October 1963), pp. 476–7. By the same author, "Essai sur la mentalité religieuse du milieu chrétien", in *Catéchèse* (July 1961), pp. 389–98.

of God's message. Because catechesis places new forms of knowledge side by side with what has been already acquired, it often
appears to be useless and even harmful for Christian life—like
some ill-digested food that "lies heavy on the stomach". One of
the signs of the authenticity of catechesis is it should tend to unify
and simplify.[4] This is also one of its urgent requirements at the
present time, since it is confronted with the many kinds of knowledge to be obtained from the mass-media. These tend, of course,
to be divisive and require to be dominated by the mind, and
criticized and unified.

Simplicity implies a balance of parts, each receiving precisely
its proper place: catechesis will not reduce everything to the same
level but will be able to distinguish what is essential from what
is only secondary, what is of faith from what is only common
teaching or mere hypothesis. Grace is more important than sin,
the Holy Spirit is more important than the pope, Christ is more
central than the Blessed Virgin, as she is in relation to the other
saints.

3. Developing a Real Sense of Duty and Personal Responsibility based on Love

A great number of Christians seem to be very legalistic in
outlook; they often give greater obedience to external authority
than to the Spirit. It is important for catechesis to show how the
obligation demanded of them is always that of God's call, the
Spirit's call. The law is never anything else but the external,
rational and communal expression of this spiritual requirement.
What is necessary is the spiritual understanding of the law and its
acceptance in love.[5] It is not a sense of duty but the love of Christ
and of others which can provide the Church with really active
Christians.

Because of their legalistic mentality, and also on account of the
common teaching during recent centuries on the place of the laity

---

[4] This simplification, according to Karl Rahner, is binding first of all
on theology. Cf. *Mission et grâce*, II: "Serviteurs du peuple de Dieu"
(Paris, 1963), p. 256, note 9, and p. 77, note 2.
[5] I. de la Potterie and S. Lyonnet, s.j., *La vie selon l'Esprit* (Paris, 1965),
pp. 185–95.

in the Church, these latter are very passive in their obedience. Such passivity cannot form the basis of true obedience which is a matter of judgment and the assumption of personal responsibility. Catechesis should train people to make personal decisions, not taken by others, but which are the fruit of the Spirit. Catechesis should gradually teach the baptized this mystery of personal assent in the Christian community; from it must be learned what a man's vocation is and how it is to be exercised as a freely creative act both of itself and of the community. This catechesis will train him in responsible personal judgment as regards sacramental practice, the apostolate and various concrete moral situations.

It will thus be able to restore every Christian to his rightful place in the Church and help each to discover his own special gift (1 Cor. 12. 4–13).

4. *Respect for Mysteries and for Concrete Reality*

Catechesis, with all the statements and explanations that go to make it up, which preserve clarity and accuracy while at the same time attempting to be meaningful, must never depart from or cause minds to lose hold of the reality of the Christian mystery and the reality of the mystery of man.

Catechesis is only commentary, the grasping by the mind, in a more or less "rational" way, of the kerygma. By the kerygma is meant the essential mystery of the love of God for us in Christ Jesus, who took flesh, died and rose again, who lives on now and whose judgment is already at work for each one of us and for all men, who requires of us conversion and liberation for a life in the Spirit.

Catechesis must always convey the impression that it is the proclamation of a concrete event, an actual mystery and an actual call to life according to the Spirit. The kerygma, the kernel of all catechesis, must be seen to appear through even the most didactic commentaries. We have suffered too much in the past from an excessive intellectualism and the memory of it is still to be found at work among us as evidenced by the anti-intellectualism of the present day. There is no separation of catechesis from life, any more than there is between arithmetic and the purchases made by any housewife; catechesis merely gives an insight into

Christian life so that it is better understood and as a result better lived. But catechesis must never be remote from the actual life of men. The divine leaven is thrown into the human dough and it is this which must rise, that is, the life of Christians, as it actually is: the life of the laity set in the midst of the compromise and ambiguity of the world and conditioned by it, family and professional life with its concrete relationships bringing both joys and sufferings—it is this life which is worked upon by the Spirit and it is with this life that the Christian, personally and with the help of others, must respond to the Spirit. Our catechesis must always strive, therefore, to be fully in touch with the concrete conditions under which the catechized live and with the concrete aspect which the kingdom of God assumes for them.

5. *Dynamism of Faith*

Our times are times of movement. We are carried along in a world in which everything seems in the melting pot and is continually changing—social classes, professions, whole ways of life, patterns of thought, successive reorganizations.[6] These changes also affect the structures of faith and of the Church. Now it is difficult indeed for one's thinking, one's faith to be in process of movement without its creating tension, disquiet and unbalance. Man, since he is continually being pushed forward, looks more to the future than to the past; under this impulse he tends to neglect the traditional so that he can try to adapt himself to the requirements of the present.

The new needs of catechesis are clearly to be seen. No longer can it claim to pass on knowledge that is to be acquired once and for all; like secular education, it must rather teach how to learn, train in self-criticism and the need for continual restatement and revision. It must be the education of a faith that is capable of finding nourishment from every experience that life brings. Christians need a living faith which is continually developing through grace and the totality of human experience. Catechesis must enable the Christian to discover for himself as he goes along the

[6] Cf. *Gaudium et spes*. This Constitution on the Church in the Modern World begins by pointing out the profound changes in the human condition, the hopes and anxieties to which these changes give rise and the difficulty of discerning the permanent values to be safeguarded.

actual solutions to the problems of his life. The catechist will give a formation leading to this discovery of judgments of faith, by himself, following a method of teaching which acts as an encouragement to the pursuit and discovery of these solutions of faith. Catechesis will also show, as was mentioned above, how a better distinction can be made between what is essential and what is less so in the content of faith, its substance and formulations; it will explain how faith remains in a state of constant and humble inquiry, how it can be enriched and purified by objections; in this way it will assist the attitude of trust, prudence and also openness and daring in faith, which must be the attitude of the Christian at the present time.

Catechesis must never give the impression that it is speaking only of past events, that it turns man's eyes towards the past. Christ rose again and is living now; it is faith which makes him really present. The kingdom of God is here; we are engaged upon the building up of the body of Christ and look forward to the parousia. The Church is prophetic and looks towards her final fulfilment. Even tradition is not static; it is incorporated in the Church as she moves forward, just as everyone takes with them their own past experiences; communion, which is the sacrament of our attitude of faith, is the viaticum for this journey.

6. *Positive and Constructive Character*

It must be emphasized further that catechesis must always proclaim good news, the peace and joy of Christ. A certain aggressive and negative way of presenting the message amounts to profound infidelity to the word of God. We must talk much more about the love of God than about sin, much more about the salvation of God than about the punishments awaiting the sinner. Only too often in our catechesis there is a tendency to present a sad and negative Christianity, one that is legalistic and minimizing, with greater emphasis on mortification and penance than on praise, joyful endeavour and thanksgiving. Of course there must be no hiding or lessening of the mystery of sin or that of the Cross. Nevertheless, the final result of our catechesis must remain good news, that is, Gospel.

At this point I must conclude the list of characteristics that our catechesis should manifest. Perhaps I have said enough to show clearly what it should be like if it is to obtain an audience among people today.

Translated by Lancelot Sheppard

Adolf Exeler

Education and Catechetics

IT IS impossible to treat the Word of God as if it were part of an educational system. It calls into question man himself and everything he does, in education as well. Karl Barth put it rather bluntly when he said: "The great breakdown can no longer be mended; it is now a matter of saints and swine." For a long time, many theologians—particularly those influenced by dialectical theology—have repeatedly and seriously warned against turning faith into a matter of education.[1] It is therefore interesting that Ratzinger, a dogmatic theologian, prefaces his *Introduction to Christianity* with the hope that it might help people to "understand faith afresh as something which makes possible true humanity in the world today".[2] This is not to gainsay Barth's "breakdown", but it would appear that its locus should be more exactly defined. The faith does not turn against what is human, but only against human self-sufficiency, and particularly against a curtailment of what is human through sheer indolence and a lack of openness.

I. THE AFFINITY BETWEEN FAITH AND EDUCATION

Faith and education aim to encourage man to be human. Clearly education consists essentially in encouraging a humanity

[1] See Reinhard Dross, *Religionsunterricht und Verkündigung. Systematische Begründung der katechetischen Praxis seit der Dialektischen Theologie* (Hamburg, 1964).
[2] J. Ratzinger, *An Introduction to Christianity* (London, 1969), Preface.

that holds out indefinite possibilities, at least in principle. Man's surplus of an overpowering, unspecified driving force and the adaptability of this driving force which distinguishes man from the animal[3] show that, in principle, man's possibilities are indefinite. Man is basically a restless and dissatisfied creature. He always wants more, and only the more and the greater can satisfy him.

The task of education is to help man to pass from this originally aimless dissatisfaction into something more constructive, and thus to achieve an existence that is worthy of him. But he will not find it in adapting himself to any situation with the least possible friction. Education is not training people for conformity, even though it often works out that way. On the contrary, many people who are outwardly wholly adapted have been ruined by this misunderstanding of education. There is a kind of education which systematically undermines the legitimate expression of a child's vitality, so that it shrivels up in the end. These children then become "difficult" because they never dare be themselves.[4] They become a burden to themselves and then to others, because they have not been able to find themselves and so suffer from a lack of fulfilment.

No doubt education must help man to let himself be guided by his own limitations, but it must also constantly encourage him to overcome them. It must enable him to avoid the various ways that lead to self-alienation. It must stimulate man's urge never to be satisfied with the given situation, never to accept it uncritically and to let himself be wholly moulded by it. On the contrary, it should make man reach out towards always greater possibilities.

When the message of faith is approached without prejudice, it is seen to have many features that are identical with education proper. Unfortunately, so far catechetics has only paid little attention to this. It is therefore useful to look at some presentations of Christianity which have no educational intention but could be of

[3] Cf. Arnold Gehlen, *Der Mensch. Seine Natur und Stellung in der Welt* (4th edn., Bonn, 1950), pp. 60–5 and 385–400.
[4] Cf. H. Müller-Eckhard, *Erziehung ohne Zwang. Kritik der Wunschbildpädagogik* (Freiburg, 1962).

surprising significance for an educational orientation of catechetics. Such a work is Ratzinger's, already mentioned.

Religious education and catechetics ought to try, in spite of the
inherent difficulties, to use the insights found in this work and
elsewhere for instruction in the faith and religious education.
What, for instance, Ratzinger says about the notion of "person"[5]
is immensely important not only for an orthodox teaching but
for an education that would break through the constrictive effects
of individualism. The person, as the realization of relation and
surrender, the interaction of supreme individuality and supreme
unity, seen in the concrete in the encounter with the specific man
Jesus,[6] is of immense educational importance.

The same holds for the community of faith we call the Church.
If to be a Christian is more than accidentally belonging to a
group, and rather a "turning towards a truly human existence",[7]
the community of Christians must be a genuine opportunity for
the building of a human community. When and in so far as the
Church is this, it will be what it ought to be. The confession of
the one God, in witness to whom many Christians have shed
their blood in the course of the centuries, was not concerned with
an isolated religious phenomenon, still less with narrow-minded
fanaticism, but with a decisive and, for the humanization of man,
most important rejection of a total absolutism of political power,
which ultimately proclaimed man's basic freedom.[8]

What I have pointed out here by referring to only one dogmatic
study, should influence our catechetics. Unfortunately, the positive boosting of the human element is badly lacking in current
catechetical practice. Catechetics and Christian education have
mainly worked in favour of a domestic in-group. They concen-
trated for too long on indoctrination, good behaviour and conformity, and steered clear of basic scepticism.

Their alienation from genuine pedagogics was brought about,
not so much by the desire to save the Word of God from becoming a questionable instrument of education, as by the total misunderstanding of what education is really about, and therefore
of what catechetics is about—since it is related to education, properly understood.

[5] J. Ratzinger, *op. cit.*
[7] *Ibid.*, p. 279.
[6] *Ibid.*, pp. 189–97.
[8] *Ibid.*, pp. 79–83.

There is a kind of instruction in the faith and a kind of education which consider themselves Christian but show their unchristian approach in a neglect of the human element. Such an education "organizes" the Christian way of life in a way which not only jeopardizes true humanization, but falls short of it. The true unfolding of morality and nobility, for instance, is often enough smothered by a morality of anxiety and by legalism. The warding-off of evil (or what is thought to be evil) frequently ousts the joy of doing what is right and good.[9]

More important still is the fact that religious education and catechetics have largely failed to bother about pedagogics at all. But when we neglect a sound pedagogical orientation, there is the danger that catechetics will fail, not only at some specific points, but throughout, and in a twofold manner: reduced on the one hand to indoctrination, and on the other to mere ritual moral training. Fortunately, both are increasingly rejected by the young, although usually only after great harm has already been done.

II. Serving the Faith, and Full Humanization

In many places one still finds a dangerously narrow concept of the function of catechetics. People are satisfied if the catechism and the Bible are "known" and those who are called "faithful" because of this knowledge "practise" their religion, i.e., obey external rules and regulations, perform certain rites and follow certain customs.

In this way, however, catechetics and so-called religious education become an obstacle to the genuine unfolding of a living faith and a religious life. For then knowledge and some external actions occupy the place of what they should lead to. They hide the real thing of which they ought to be only the expression. This real thing is the life with God which is only true life if it pervades the whole of man's existence.

The tendency to pursue religious knowledge and ritualism for their own sake is not exactly a new phenomenon in Christianity.

[9] Cf. O. Betz, *Zumutung des Glaubens. Ansätze für die religiöse Erziehung angesichts eines neuen Glaubensverständnisses* (Munich, 1968), pp. 46–55, 69–74.

It is as old as the faith itself, and must therefore be constantly exposed and resisted. We find that prophets fought it when, for instance, they turned against a ritualistic penitential system which encouraged people to hope that they could be reconciled with God through religious practices instead of genuine conversion. We find it also in Jesus' conflict with some groups among his contemporaries that put external religious practice above an authentic inner life.

The unmasking of this diminution of religious life will always remain one of the tasks of ecclesiastical renewal. These features are the most subtle obstacle to religious life because this busying oneself about religion can easily cover up the real failures in life, and because those who want to purge this religious practice are often accused of being enemies of religion and of the faith. We should not forget that Jesus was put to death by very pious people in the name of God and for the sake of religion.[10]

Genuine Christian catechetics must be conducted so that it really serves the faith and, by necessary implication, the humanization of man. If a child comes to know the so-called "faith" only as a lot of puzzling statements that have to be learnt by heart together with a lot of precepts and prohibitions, unbelief will be the eventual result.[11]

When a child cannot avoid the impression that the main purpose of religion is to make him "behave", so that adults will not be annoyed and the "dear God" and his representatives will approve of him, it is hardly astonishing that a lively young person simply does not want to be religious in this sense. The faith is often abandoned because man wants freedom and autonomy. When a young person does not experience that living with God is precisely a matter of freedom and autonomy, a basically free gift, an appeal to his humanity and an unfolding of all his powers, the creative ones included, we must expect him one day to tear through this suffocating straitjacket of the religious and moral behaviour expected of him. He will find that religion has deceived him where his humanity is concerned.[12]

---

[10] Cf. E. Käsemann, *Der Ruf der Freiheit* (2nd edn., Tübingen, 1968), pp. 28–58.

[11] Cf. O. Betz, *op. cit.*, pp. 14–20.

[12] Cf. M. Oraison, *Love or Constraint* (London, 1959).

An education which believes in the creative spirit and accepts that man's unending future has already set in in Christ Jesus must break down the barriers which confine him to a fenced-off garden plot. It must try to evoke the creative element and the power of imaginative discovery, for the sake of God and man, the spirit of enterprise and the will to conquer in the name of God.

III. Interaction of Experience and Concrete Expression of Faith

Every human being has to mature in a lifelong process of growth. This process inevitably implies a number of crises which demand that he constantly start afresh. Growth in the faith is no exception to this rule. That is why it is so important for those in charge of the religious education of the young to understand the natural pre-conditions of the faith and to take them seriously. These pre-conditions are too often neglected.

A young person who has so little experience of being trusted that he trusts no one, will not be able to bring himself to believe in God. When a man resents his fate, is embittered, and has never managed to say "thank you" honestly, this pre-conditioning makes him unable to take a genuine part in the Eucharist. These two examples ought to be enough to show that the growth of man's experience and his basic attitudes to faith constantly influence each other.

Although the faith is always one, the provisional character of the pre-existing conditions must constantly be overcome and make room for new perspectives. This is because the faith is not a collection of truths that can be learnt quickly but a new way of life, in which a man is gradually drawn into a relationship with God and into the movement of the people of God in the course of history.

The fullness of the life that man is offered here can only unfold itself as he advances into it, step by step. Just as a child cannot be defined as a small adult, and infancy and adolescence are specific stages in the one life of man, so the faith of a child is not an abridged edition of the faith of an adult. It is a faith that corresponds to the specific stage reached in life; it becomes inadequate whenever one tries to preserve it without any elaboration exactly as one experienced it in a previous stage of life. In contrast to the way in which faith is still so often spoken about in catechetics, Scripture rarely talks about "keeping" or "losing" the faith, but very often about the need to grow constantly in the faith.[13] One cannot "keep" the faith; one can only let it come to full fruition or allow it to perish.

The catechist must be fully alert and sensitive to these phases of development if he wants to be of use to people according to the situation in which they find themselves. The ability and readiness to go on learning is increasingly an important factor in society. Therefore instruction and education should abandon the attempt to cling to a fixed and static position which would remain normative for the rest of a person's life.

Instruction and education should open up fields where decisions can be taken freely, and should help entry into these fields. The form which the faith takes in a particular person depends on his condition and his specific phase in life, and is therefore relative. The growth of a man's faith necessarily changes the quality of this faith with his growth in experience of life and deeper understanding of himself and the world.[14]

IV. URGENT TASKS FOR CATECHETICS

The problem created for catechetics by the constantly changing shape of the faith is still unsolved, in spite of some efforts. It would no doubt be agreeable if we could simply say what topics should be chosen for instruction and what texts of the Bible would be most suitable for a particular age-group; if we could show how the aspects of belief in Jesus as the Christ shift normally, or when one can speak meaningfully about "guilt" and "sin".

---

[13] Cf. 1 Cor. 3. 1; 13. 11; 14. 20; Eph. 4. 13 ff.; Phil. 1. 9; Col. 1. 9 f.; 1 Thess. 3. 12; 4. 10; 1 Peter 3. 10.

[14] For the various forms of faith, see, for instance: A. Exeler, *Glaube an Jesus, den Christus. Unser Dienst am Christusglauben der heutigen Jugend* (Freiburg, 1968); A. Liégé, *Adultes dans le Christ* (Brussels, 2nd edn., 1960); H. Spaemann, *Orientierung am Kinde* (Düsseldorf, 1967).

But study of the elements of catechetics which concern the psychology of growth is still initial and hypothetical.[15]

In general, the idea has now been abandoned that the 14-year-old must be told all that is essential for an understanding of Christianity for the rest of his life. Although much has been done to adapt to age where children and adolescents are concerned, nobody has yet pinned down the specific impulses and motive forces of various age-groups so that they clearly correspond to the development of faith.

Yet it is precisely this kind of assessment which is necessary if the faith is to become the liberating response to man's deepest desires, which often are still inarticulated but determine the course of life. Without this, it is almost impossible to experience the faith as an aid to humanization, and instruction in the faith, despite all attempts to modernize it, would remain the intrusion of an alien world.

In the meantime, other elements have emerged together with the psychology of growth; these are concerned with the typical features of an epoch—the historical changes in mentality which religious instruction can ignore only at its peril.[16] The study of modern youth might offer many suggestions.[17]

Beyond this psychology of growth and the historical change of mentality catechetics should examine the nature of faith as a process. It must be studied, not only as it develops in the individual, but in the awareness of the whole believing community.

This process passes beyond the psychology of growth and

[15] Here one could mention the whole controversy about the "progressive catechism". For the most recent contributions see J. Colomb, *Le service de l'Evangile. Manuel catéchétique* (Paris, 1968), I, pp. 193–328 ("Fidélité à l'homme"); II, pp. 245–456 ("La Catéchèse aux divers âges de l'homme"); J. Dreissen, *Grundlinien heutiger Katechese* (Munich, 1967); O. and F. Betz, *Stationen des Glaubens* (Freiburg, 1965).

[16] Cf. P. Babin, *Les jeunes et la foi* (Lyon, 1963); E. Feifel, *Die Glaubensunterweisung und der abwesende Gott. Not und Zuversicht der Katechese im Kraftfeld des Unglaubens* (Freiburg, 1965); J. Colomb, *op. cit.*, II, pp. 457–572.

[17] For an introduction to this problem, see D. Ausubel, *Das Jugendalter* (Munich, 1965); H. Giesecke, *Jungsein in Deutschland* (Munich, 1967—bibl.); H. Halbfas, *Jugend und Kirche* (Düsseldorf, 1965); A. Flitner, *Glaubensfragen im Jugendalter* (Heidelberg, 1961); Viggo Graf Blücher, *Die Generation der Unbefangenen* (Düsseldorf, 1966).

knowledge of modern youth, and leads to important problems of pastoral theology and therefore also of catechetics. Religious instruction must make it a conscious process so that the faithful rise, actually or potentially, above the passive consumption of an already static faith to become active partners in the fostering of awareness of the faith.

Hence catechetics today can no longer take the faith for granted. It must realize that many of those who receive instruction will never reach the true faith and sound Christian practice, or will remain static. But if catechetics is understood as an aid to humanization, it may still mean much to many who do not get beyond a vague and somewhat sceptical sympathy for the faith and the Church.

Catechetics cannot avoid a demand for decisions. But this demand should not be made at too early a stage, and the decisions asked for should not be merely negative. Decisions taken by children and adolescents are usually very specific and concrete, and it is important that the way to a whole series of new decisions should remain open.

Translated by Theo Westow

Karl Ernst Nipkow

Beyond the Bible in Religious Education

I. Scripture

IN THE Protestant Church (in Germany at least) the traditional divisions of religious education are scripture, doctrine and church history. The Bible is the basic tool of school R.E., whereas candidates for confirmation are prepared mainly by instruction in the most important sections of the catechism and divine service. Hymn singing is also a significant feature. In general, Catholic religious education displays the same emphases. Catechetics obviously means more than scripture teaching, but are the problems of an appropriate methodology to be raised only in terms of church history, doctrine and liturgy? Is the Bible part straightforward? Is the best possible catechetics of the future to be worked out by re-planning the non-biblical area, or should we be working out wholly new methods and themes? Does the present debate on catechetics offer any hints about the right way to take?

Scripture has become increasingly important in Catholic R.E. in the last few years. This favourable development has also affected official syllabuses. For example, the basic religious syllabus authorized by the German bishops indicates that the Bible is of primary importance: "All instruction apart from direct scriptural catechesis must proceed in the spirit of the Bible."[1] This development has been considerably influenced by the evolution of hermeneutical theory in Evangelical theology, and by the concentration of Evangelical religious education on biblical exegesis

[1] Munich, 1967, pp. 42 and 8.

as the fundamental form of instruction.[2] Yet this central emphasis on the Bible and its interpretation as *the* basic form of religious education has been the very point to be called in question in the most recent discussion of the subject within the Evangelical Church.[3]

Study of the Catholic situation also shows that an attempt is being made to shift the emphasis in catechetics, even before the influence of scripture scholarship on religious education has had the universal practical results that are so requisite. Of course objections are raised against certain dangers to be expected in "catechetical exegesis",[4] but the new movement goes beyond such plaints. Even the above-mentioned syllabus shows signs of the main concern, which is to achieve the decisive effects of religious education not through instruction but through "practice"—an integral process in liturgy, church life and Christian behaviour.[5] Is religious education ideally to be a neat conjunction of the "cognitive" processes of understanding and learning on the one hand, and the concomitant and subsequent fulfilment of behaviour on the other, with the emphasis on "affective" and "pragmatic" processes?

There is a universal trend nowadays (not least in modern theology) towards the union of theory and practice; theoretical assertions have to be tested in life situations. Educationists proper as well as religious educationists are concerned to develop means of stimulating appropriate attitudes as well as the right kind of awareness in young people; they are also anxious to encourage satisfactory behavioural motivation. One wonders, however, whether the religious lesson in school is the right place for

[2] See particularly the publications of H. Halbfas, A. Höfer, W. Langer and G. Stachel.

[3] H.-B. Kaufmann, "Mue die Bibel im Mittelpunkt des Religionsunterrichts stehen?", in *Schule und Kirche vor den Aufgaben der Erziehung*, ed. G. Otto and H. Stock (Hamburg, 1968), pp. 79–83; K. E. Nipkow, "Christlicher Glaubensunterricht in der Säkularität—Die zwei didaktischen Grundtypen des evangelischen Religionsunterrichts", in *Der Evangelischer Erzieher*, 20 (1968), pp. 169–89.

[4] W. Nastainczyk, "Katechetischer Exegetismus im Kommen oder Vergehen?", in *Katechetische Blätter*, 94 (1969), pp. 56–63.

[5] *Op. cit.*, 7, 12, 19 *passim*, cf. *Einführung in den Rahmenplan*, ed. H. Fischer (Munich, 1967), pp. 44, 57 ff.; a critical assessment of the foregoing is available: E. Meueler in *Theologia Practica*, 4 (1969), p. 294.

liturgical education in the practical sense. When young Protestants were asked to look back on their schooldays and say what they thought about the value of prayer and song in their religious education, the majority of the sample (77%) were against their use.[6] Anyway, the right direction in which to pursue the question of adding to teaching from the Bible would seem to be the relationship of faith and reality.

II. Determining Factors of R.E.

To turn religious instruction into worship is just as questionable as fanatical scripture study; nevertheless judicious choice and application of the themes of Christian religious education ought to be determined in the light of the scriptural origins and the contemporary practice of the Church.

Christian religious education must relate to a considerable extent to the given derivation and reality of faith, if it is to retain its character as initiation into Christian belief, and if it is not to become the mere imparting of general religious knowledge.

Nevertheless, the factors that determine religious curricula and specific themes, contents and methods are not wholly restricted by ecclesiastical and theological considerations and requirements emanating "from the Church". It is much more important that the theory of religious education, which is co-determined by pedagogical suasions, should be worked out in full consciousness of the fact that "Christian" education (the efforts of the Church to instruct and educate young people) isn't just factually and inevitably connected with "general education", but has expressly to relate to the contemporary experience and future concerns and pursuits of the younger generation—for the sake of their future, and for their own sake as Christians *and* as human beings living in the world of the present.[7] The religious educator as educator might require, in accordance with contemporary general educational theory, the themes of religious education to be discovered

[6] According to a still unpublished survey by the Protestant Church in the Pfalz area of the Federal Republic.

[7] The Churches are responsible not only for "Christian education" within the Church, but for "general education": World Council of Churches/World Council of Christian Education, *The Final Report of the Joint Study Commission on Education, 1964-1968* (Geneva, 1968).

in the context of the ultimately unenforceable development of young people's ideas, expectations and convictions—a development that, despite the need for guidance and instruction, cannot be simply determined in advance. The religious educator as theologian, however, might plead just as resolutely—on behalf of the Church—the question of theological presuppositions governing the nature of the religious education offered to young people, and might, indeed, raise the general problem of the nature of the fundamental relationship between faith (in the sense of belief) and the world. A form of catechetics that might be called both educationally and theologically responsible takes shape only at the point where these convergent (or divergent) determinants intersect.

III. Faith and the "Non-Christian" World

I shall refer only briefly to what seems educationally significant in the opinions of those who are actually on the receiving end of catechetical instruction. Numerous investigations—old and new—of young people's expectations and requirements show the firm demand of those between thirteen and nineteen for instruction in Christian belief that is unmistakably relevant to life as it is actually experienced, and that doesn't fight shy of criticism and questioning of traditional material.

Catholic research among Protestant and Catholic secondary school children from sixteen to nineteen in the Frankfurt–Wiesbaden area of West Germany showed at the pilot study stage that pupils of both denominations without distinction unequivocally relegated Bible, doctrine and church history—the traditional tools of religious instruction—to second place. Instead, they wanted the areas of "sociology of religion", "basic religious philosophies and comparative religion", and "problems of everyday life (social behaviour)", to be given pride of place.[8] Apparently Christian belief should be presented not as a structure separate from life as it really is, and as an intrinsically ecclesiastical and immanent system, but as coming to grips with the sociology of religion, philosophical criticism and the relativizations of the

[8] J. Fuhrmann, *Religionsunterricht in der Höheren Schule* (Diocesan Youth Dept., Limburg, 1958), p. 21.

scientific study of religion—which the truth of faith might well be able to contest, but which the faith in all its truth ought to prove of value and might well accept as true.

The desire to examine Christian belief in conjunction with other forms of the search for truth and other philosophies of life is apparent, in parallel to the above-mentioned investigation, in the survey of young Protestant opinion I have already referred to (cf. n. 6). A very considerable majority of students in the upper secondary school wanted more time to be given to philosophy and the analysis of modern literature during religious instruction. Half the respondents still found the interpretation of passages from the Gospel of interest, and more than half thought that Church history had some place in the religious lesson.

The shift of preference in this investigation (carried out in the Pfalz area) is strikingly similar to that apparent in the Frankfurt survey. The Bible and Church history, which are traditional components of religious instruction, should still be considered important; but the way in which the message of the Bible is expressed and put over ought to be changed. The "themes" and "materials" to be used apart from the Bible in catechesis are not just other theological or ecclesiastical phenomena; instead, all these traditional theological and ecclesiastical (i.e., biblical, dogmatic, moral-theological, church-historical and liturgical) themes should come into contact with non-theological and non-ecclesiastical themes and matter. As far as young people are concerned, the revision of a syllabus of Christian religious education should not be restricted to a new arrangement of Christian themes, but ought to go beyond their limits by decisively taking up the reality of "non-Christian life" and relating it to Christian belief.

The import of this for catechetical method is that much greater use than hitherto must be made of documents and other materials from the "profane" world: recourse should be had to short stories, novels and poems, radio and other plays,[9] memoirs and letters, essays and reportage, pop and protest songs, eye-witness reports and statistics, children's own creative and discursive writing,

---

[9] Cf. F. Hahn, *Moderne Literatur im kirchlichen Unterricht* (Munich, 1963); *Bibel und moderne Literatur* (Stuttgart, 1967).

visual aids from the most diverse sources, and so on, and so on. . . .[10]

IV. THEOLOGICAL FUNCTION OF SECULAR LIFE-THEMES

Of course it will be objected that even if young people express this kind of desire the message of the Bible doesn't necessarily require such a confrontation if it's to get through. It will be said, too, that non-biblical and non-ecclesiastical themes are suitable only at an advanced stage of religious instruction, and that older pupils are already provided for in terms of so-called "life-themes", particularly in the more recent syllabuses. The second point would be made with some justice since, in Germany anyway, the 1968 syllabus recommends the use of secular life-themes quite early on: to some extent from the sixth and then decisively from the seventh, but most emphatically and adequately in the ninth school year.[11] In the Protestant syllabuses of religious education, the discussion of faith and life using "profane" documents and text begins at the latest in the ninth school year.

But is this enough? Above all, doesn't this introduction of life-themes at what is still a very late stage indicate something that is also revealed in the overall structure of catechesis (first of all, between six and eight years of age, an introduction to intrinsically ecclesiastical, "spiritual" themes in an enclosed world, and *only then* the "spiritual themes seen in relation to "worldly" themes)? It shows that reality is thought of as a "field of application" for the faith, and at best as a point of contact; but in both cases essentially as something that doesn't belong to the nature of faith from the start. We must ask if the salvific reality experienced in faith can be expressed and taught in catechesis as a self-sufficient structure without any reference to mundane reality. The Old and the New Testaments would provide the answer No. Anyway, the full consequences and basic implications of the relationship

---

[10] The most important materials for this kind of work are appropriate collections of texts, and work-books. E.g., *Lesebuch für den Religionsunterricht*, ed. M. Hartenstein *et al.*, two vols. (Stuttgart, 1969); H. Blessenohl, *Erkenne-entscheide, Arbeitsbuch für den kath. Religionsunterricht in der Realschule* (Düsseldorf, 1968).

[11] Cf. especially the selection of themes, pp. 77 ff., and also the *Katechetische Beiheft zum Rahmenplan* (ninth school year) (Munich, 1968).

between faith and reality are not yet known for every form of proclamation and catechesis.

Certain tendencies of recent Protestant and Catholic theology
can help us responsibly and fundamentally to assess the educational and theological expansion and revision of religious education. Above all it is important to recognize that any talking about
God—in R.E. as well—is a matter of responsibility before God.
And the only way in which this responsibility can be realized is
before the world.[12] Which doesn't mean just tacking the world on
or slipping it in as an afterthought.

Gerhard Ebeling stresses the fact that this kind of mundane responsibility isn't a task that comes in second place after talking
about God, but a part of God-talk from the start. God's revelation
is fulfilled in historical reality, which is comprehensible and
accessible for men as the actual life lived by men on this earth.
"I just can't responsibly accept something that isn't evidently and
comprehensibly related to the experiences I can have in the real
world" (ibid., p. 356). The question of where proclamation and
catechesis can be effective is therefore a question of where men
actually live their lives, and a question of whether what's going
to be said to them is something they'll actually be able to understand. The area of effectiveness is man's contemporary understanding of himself and the world—which involves radical questioning: "Whoever refuses questions has no idea what the word
'God' means" (ibid.).

What does this imply? Obviously that it would be wrong to
preach the Gospel as an a-historical and therefore extra-mundane
truth. It has to be proclaimed so that man's bearings to himself
and to the world consciously allow the conjunction of the word
of God and historical (i.e., existential) reality. It is not only the
"task of theology" to "develop the knowledge of God in terms
of a correlation of understanding of the world and self-under-
standing",[13] for the tasks and themes of religious education issue
from this correlation as well.

It is important in this field not to stay in the realm of the

---

[12] G. Ebeling, Wort und Glaube (Tübingen, 1962), p. 374. (English trans.:
Word and Faith [Fortress Press, 1963].)

[13] J. Moltmann, Theologie der Hoffnung (Munich, 1968), p. 57. (English
trans.: Theology of Hope [London, 1968].)

general and the abstract; and existential hermeneutics above all is accused nowadays of exclusive generalization and abstraction. God revealed himself as the existential word in the history of the people of Israel, in the proclamation of Jesus and in the primitive Christian kerygma. He addressed the people of the Old and the New Covenants in their real (which means too in their social and political) lives, in order to promise them an alteration of this life —beginning now. The Church proclaims the reality of salvation as something that has already dawned, and continues to proclaim the promise of its fulfilment. She has to do this ever and again in the same sort of *actual* way that it was done long ago; she has to do it straightforwardly, and to do it for human beings whose experience and questioning are mediated in a wholly historical and social manner.

Therefore there are *two* basic questions for the Church in preaching and instruction. One is: What did the men who wrote the Bible mean when they wrote their particular bits of it? Therefore the Bible is unconditionally part of Christian preaching and Christian religious instruction. The other question is: What are the latent and obvious problems of young people and adults that could still be answered by what the authors of the Bible meant at the time of writing? This searching out of the ever-changing questions of men—right up to what is radically questionable—is so important that such secular life-themes cannot be peripherally "thematized" as "supplementary" material or examples for "contrasting".[14]

In the process of religious education, the tradition of Christian belief handed down to us and now continuing, *and* contemporary reality, must be approached and related with equal seriousness and intensity. The teacher of religion who, say, spends several hours with his pupils in elucidating a fragment of experience relevant to and for his pupils, and in examining its various aspects and associated assumptions (for example, the ways in which the

[14] G. Otto, *Handbuch des Religionsunterrichts* (Hamburg, 1964), pp. 256–261; cf. however G. Otto, *"Der Mensch* in seiner Welt"*, in *Theologica Practica* (1967); according to Otto "the anthropological dimension in the widest sense" should be brought into religious education, and "a new relationship between biblical and 'non-biblical' contents is requisite in religious education and also between religious education and all other subjects".

children in the class actually experience fear and anxiety, and the ways in which adults today know fear and anxiety), is not allowing himself to be sidetracked from the mystery of faith "itself". Is not, precisely because he's searching for the area where the Christian faith as it's been handed down can be made comprehensible, and is therefore getting closer and closer to the truth of faith.

In recent Protestant and Catholic theology, the insight is becoming increasingly clear that the exact analysis of existential and social reality does not lead theology away from but towards what is proper to it, and does so in a way that is necessarily novel; if this weren't so, theology would be without the necessary possibility of actual, relevant talk about God. Ebeling justly requires "a comprehensive analysis of reality—which can't be universally valid for all time" to attend to "reality's radical openness to questioning" (op. cit., p. 366). Such a demand for a comprehensive analysis of things as they are also requires an assessment of the theoretical and practical tasks that are still before the Church (in catechetics as well).

The analysis of reality as the presupposition of concrete, socially relevant proclamation on the part of the Church demands, among other things, the "consideration and digestion of *data* that are more than just the results of ecclesiastical and theological reflections".[15] Every teacher of religion has to concern himself with these data of reality in the form of secular documentation and texts, and of unceasing direct observation. Otherwise his religious teaching will be stuck in the miniature ghetto of piety for its own sake. "A fear of everything that even imperceptibly smacks of thought about the world and impertinent inquiry into the nature of faith is strong" in some Evangelical theologies.[16] As Metz stresses, the Church and theology have to find their way to men anew by means of a "hermeneutics" of the "public, socially relevant and socially effective word".[17] In the same way, in religious education the socially relevant word must be seen "not

---

[15] J. B. Metz, *Zur Theologie der Welt* (Mainz–Munich, 1968), p. 113. (English trans.: *Theology of the World* [London, 1969].)

[16] J. M. Jong, in: W.-D. Marsch (ed.), *Die Diskussion über die "Theologie der Hoffnung"* (Munich, 1967), p. 28.

[17] *Op. cit.*, p. 117.

merely as a supplementary and instrumental but as an essential and fundamental element of Christian self-expression" (*ibid.*, p. 116).

V. Instruction in "Context"

An attempt has been made to show that "secular" themes and methods are not peripheral but central to catechesis. This doesn't mean that religious education is watered down to produce only a workaday philosophy of life, or "civics". Of course some teachers of religion do wander off into this kind of lesson, having been thoroughly unsettled by R.E. as practised to date. But this would be a misunderstanding of what I'm after, which is the relationship—the connection—between faith and reality. The didactic form of the kind of "thematic instruction" I refer to is "contextual". In North Germany, particularly in Lower Saxony, as in the South (Baden–Württemberg), projects of this kind are being developed and tested for children of thirteen upwards. The themes (prejudice, libel, conflict of the generations, Christian participation in the protest movement, aggression, prayer, the peace movement) are selected, and the corresponding didactic materials and media (literary texts, visual aids, films) are presented, so that light is simultaneously thrown *both* on man as he finds himself, his questions and impulses, his conceptions of reality and truth, *and* on man who, encountering God's revelation and promise, finds his true "identity" and what he will be in terms of that promise.[18] Continually renewed analyses of reality, worked out in conjunction with the pupils, form the basis of an understanding of reality that is both critical and responsible, its raw material being the understanding contributed by the pupils themselves or one they have derived from adults; in the same process one may expect a truly critical and responsible manipulation (because it is at one and the same time a true identification of this reality) of those statements of the Bible and the Church that are brought into play.

I should like to say something more about the form of instruction in which biblical, church-historical, dogmatic and ecclesiastical materials are used in conjunction with statistics and legal

[18] J. Moltmann, *op. cit.*, p. 80.

documents, newspaper reports, personal observations, literary work and—of course—other religions and philosophies of life. It is true—though in a negative sense—that the mission of the Church should not be uncritically adapted to the world. On the other hand, the world ought not to serve merely as a dark background to set off to advantage the Christian view of life. And any analyses of reality that are undertaken ought not to be means of exemplifying the truth of faith by means of mundane evidence. The primary task is much more straightforward and generally more down to earth. It's a matter of getting to know the actual life situations of adults, and above all of the children under instruction. Of course, more or less living traditions and structures of belief form part of their life, but so do a very great number of things, all of which can only be exemplified—but by a form of generalization that is inductive (i.e., not deductive) and close to actuality. And to get to know things as they really are, the opinions, convictions, forms of behaviour and even testimonies of unbelief that obtain outside the Church must become the objects of a factual and responsible attempt to understand—i.e., to understand on the basis of their specific suppositions.[19]

In addition, as is shown by the discussions that have taken place between Christians and Marxists, at present Christian commitment and the forms of commitment peculiar to other groups are parallel. Men of very different beliefs and backgrounds stand together because their common task is the humanization of our world. This parallelism or convergence cannot be adequately emphasized unless the appropriate non-Christian materials are used together with the usual catechetical resources. And it's not enough merely to record agreement on certain points: often non-Christian testimonies prompt Christians into recognition of tasks and duties they have forgotten, or those that have been pushed to one side because of a misunderstanding of the particular mission of Christians. They remind them of their responsibility in standing up for solutions to specific social problems, and for the defence of freedom of belief and conscience; they point to *idées fixes* of the institutional Church that have long remained without critical

[19] Th. Filthaut, *Aspekte der Glaubensunterweisung von morgen* (Freiburg-Basle-Vienna, 1968), p. 27.

examination. Voices from outside the Church can awaken Christians to self-criticism—in catechesis as well.

Yet someone could object that these are not functions "proper to" the nature of religious education. The answer would be that dialogue with secular reality is a necessary and fully valid means by which faith serves the world and declares itself in the world. Unpretentiously, the Christian must seek out what lies about him, what is with him and what is against him, so that in his undemonstrative seeking and service he may be known as a witness to the good news. This mission cannot be undertaken without conflict. Therefore instruction about the faith must always be instruction about the contradiction between the Christian and the world; because the postulates of hope in the Christian promise are intended to emphasize and elucidate the reality which is "to come", they must enter into conflict with reality as it is experienced in the present.[20]

Since he who believes and lives in hope will never be able to compromise with the laws and obligations of this world, with the inevitability of death or the continuance of evil (Moltmann), the Gospel also has its own continuing and specific critical power. Accordingly the Christian, in conscious knowledge of the loving action of God that has already come to pass, and of its fulfilment in the unrest of loving and active application to the world, "overtakes contemporaneity" by means of his (i.e., God's) "future".[21] The Christian contribution to religious education in "context" therefore has not only a critical but a constantly stimulating and creative aspect. Only this ultimate perspective, with its divine Yes to the world in Jesus Christ as the basis of faith, love and hope, can make quite plain what the Gospel clearly implies.

VI. Proposals

The renewal of the themes and intentions of religious education has been considerably quickened by the post-conciliar catechetical movement. Theodor Filthaut's admirable book on the R.E. of the future (*Aspekte der Glaubensunterweisung von morgen*, 1968) is an attempt to present this "renewal of religious instruction in

---

[20] J. Moltmann, *op. cit.*, p. 13.

[21] E Rosenstock-Huessy, *Des Christen Zukunft oder Wir überholen die Moderne* (Munich, 1955).

the spirit of the Second Vatican Council". In general, Filthaut's observations agree with my own. He stresses the centrality of the Bible in all R.E., but requires its interpretation and that of Christian tradition in general to be referred to an interpretation of contemporary reality. New "secular" materials and themes come into the foreground; others are given a new emphasis: teaching about "evil in the world' and the "incomprehensibility of God", the treatment of non-Christian religions and their new evaluation, a realistic and critical examination of the particular Church to which teacher and taught belong, the Church as an historical and dynamic entity, "ecumenical education", teaching about "Christians and Jews", and "education for life in modern society"; education "for peace", instruction on the subject of "politics and salvation", and on the "inhumanity of war". These are some of the wide-ranging themes.

Because of variations in age and experience, the changing problems of children and young people can be determined only by means of repeated inquiries and surveys, and ultimately only in the actual teaching situation itself. And the fundamental emphasis on the relation between faith and experience, between faith and reality, is not to be restricted to the upper classes of the secondary school. Hubertus Halbfas has suggested the importance of fairy-stories and legends, proverbs and songs, and simple tales, for the first years of religious education.[22] But he considers that a "universally open conflict" between biblical tradition and human experience is fundamental and requisite.

Of course much deliberation will be needed to decide the changes in syllabuses necessary for different age-groups, and the form (e.g., "contextual", or purely scriptural, or purely church-historical) that is appropriate in each specific case. The need for the kind of changes I have referred to here will probably be recognized increasingly. The realization must come that—for all age-groups—the discussion of problems concerning this life, with an eye to the truth of faith, "must be considered a valid and often even the only possible form of catechesis".[23]

[22] H. Halbfas, *Fundamentalkatechetik* (Düsseldorf, 1968), pp. 299, 315.
[23] Introduction to the *Rahmenplan, op. cit.*, p. 108; cf. also O. Betz, *Die Zumutung des Glaubens* (Munich, 1968), pp. 182 ff., 148 ff.

Translated by John Griffiths

Jean Le Du

Language Problems and Catechetics

IN this article I shall deal with some of the questions raised by catechetics in relation to the young and to adults. I shall consider them from the point of view of "language". But this word does not imply only questions of terminology, vocabulary, style or rational schemes, for if it did I should be considering established language only and this article would almost necessarily take a linguistic form. On the contrary, my contention is that the problems of catechetics will emerge only if considered in terms of language at the emergent stage, of the act of communication itself; this can be done by analysing its various forms, by comparing its different processes and by emphasizing different aspects of meaning within an effective experience.

Admittedly, valuable information may be obtained by studying a text, i.e., by carefully analysing an actual catechism. I have often used this method, which is easier than an attempt to revive the experience of an act of communication; it reveals quite elementary information about the catechist and shows how, consciously or unconsciously, he regards his function and expresses in language the relationship he is trying to establish with his hearers. But exclusive recourse to this method does not reveal how the words have been *heard*. Has the attempted relationship really been understood and accepted, or refused? At once we are confronted with the language evolved by the catechist for the group, and not with the language produced by this group for its own use.

Therefore we are studying a situation in which the catechist has retained the initiative. He chooses the subjects to be dealt with, solves the problems, and decides the course to be followed; he knows where he is going. But this situation is peculiar to the catechist, and only the starting-point in discovering how to adapt our language to our audience. This more usual method is possibly not the most fruitful. When the group decides the question to be studied, its starting-point, the objective in view and the sources to be consulted, the catechist's position is quite different. A cate-chesis with this kind of internal organization entirely changes the question of a "language adapted to the audience", and en-ables us to discover not the catechist's language, but that produced by the group itself.

In the first part of this article I should like to consider these questions from the fairly limited viewpoint of the intellectual process of a group of this kind developing its own language. I shall examine them on the basis of an actual occurrence, and with reference to an effective pastoral experience.

I. How a Language Emerges

I know a group of adults who on their own initiative meet regularly to examine the meaning of their faith. Their motive is a chronic dissatisfaction with the religious language they en-counter in the pulpit or in the many periodicals and books in which the Church tries to express herself. To them, the language in which the Church talks about social questions is incurably moralistic and exhibits a facile optimism; in religious matters it is astonishingly naïve and without any critical sense. During the first meetings the remark to be heard most frequently was, "You'll never get me to believe again that. . . ." The basis of this dissatisfaction is in part the almost total meaninglessness of the most fundamental propositions of Christianity. To hold articles of faith as true no longer has any real, basic significance. "What can confession to a priest mean to people like us? What's the sense of the Church's claim to subject her faithful to this rule?"

1. *A Discussion Group on Guilt and Reconciliation*

At the third meeting of the group, after questions had been dealt with, a kind of contract was agreed to and signed by each

member. More or less explicitly this contract formed the signa-
tories into a research group; it was decided that anything which
proved an obstacle to the purpose of the group would be removed, including if necessary the catechist's interventions. The
members were thus dedicating themselves to unremitting creative
activity with regard to religious meaning; they felt entitled to
freedom "to take it or leave it". Thus a young woman expressed
the following view: "I'm quite ready to believe that Mary is
virgin and mother; but as long as the actual meaning of this statement, and its effects in my own life are not clear to me I shelve
it, so to speak. It doesn't worry me—nowadays at least. I have a
whole heap of things like that, one more or one less, you
know. . . . But what bothers me at present is the Church's attitude
towards man's guilt; it seems to me that she increases it. . . . I
should like to go into this thoroughly for my children's sake, and
because I don't want to bring them up like me."

Conversations tend to take a form such as the following: someone asks the question, "Does anyone here still go to confession?"
Subsequent admissions are often surprising: these Catholics have
almost entirely given up the sacrament of penance. There was
even a tragi-comic incident when a business man discovered from
his wife's embarrassed admission that although he still went to
confession once or twice a year at her suggestion, she didn't any
longer.

As the group's inquiries gradually take shape, they are
ultimately concerned less with sin (religious vocabulary) than
with guilt understood in the human sense; less with absolu-
tion or pardon than with reconciliation—again in the human
sense. The process seems to lead towards a possible meaning for
religious terms. This is both less and more than might be thought.
The key terms admitted from the outset, probably because they
are heavily loaded with experience, are guilt and reconciliation.
The realities of guilt are discussed exhaustively from the indirect
angle of the education of children ("they mustn't be given com-
plexes"), and an approach is made to the way that each one
struggles with his responsibilities, his failings and the burden of
his conscience.

Time is needed for the various shades of meaning of the term
"guilt" to gain acceptance; it must come to be recognized that

it is not discreditable nor even pathological to feel guilt; that perhaps it is a human characteristic not to escape guilt but to accept and control it. Very different opinions are met with, like that of Fourastié: "I do not feel any more guilty at being obliged to live under an unjust economic system than at being forced to live in a world in which cyclones kill grasshoppers, or men kill sheep, or where the nights are not the same length as the days. . . ." Or there is the widespread opinion: "We are all murderers really. . . ."

Although the discussion is at a fairly general and theoretical level, the members of the group feel that they are all involved in a personal dilemma; that each is trying to discover what provokes the thought: "You are not up to the level of your capabilities; you are living only to the half of your powers; you are failing yourself and others."

A number of questions arise and are more or less adequately formulated: "Why can't we live without doing wrong?" wonders a business man whose ideal of social justice is constantly refuted by his professional conduct. "What are we hoping for when we try to get members of a family to be quite open with each other?" asks a wife whose moral idealism is sorely tried by her older, adolescent children who are gradually drawing further away and so harming family unity. "Don't you think that religion increases men's guilt?" asks a young student, who reads us a passage from Nietzsche in support of his assertion.

And so the general trend is towards self-reconciliation—badly needed even though the way to it is yet to be found. The important question becomes: "How can we manage to live with this lack of balance within ourselves? How can we avoid suffering too much from our inevitable wrong-doing, without destroying the whole basis of our moral life, or giving way to the illusion of idealism? What attitude are we to adopt to past actions which we now repudiate since we can no longer recognize ourselves in them? Are we to forgot them, and if so, what will become of them? Won't they torture us secretly from outside? Wouldn't it be better to be in touch with our whole life, including our sins, and be in a position to acknowledge them like any other actions of our past?"

This quest for an art of living develops and is deepened through personal testimony; gradually it can be seen how greatly each individual values these ways of reconciliation, down to the smallest details of daily life—like the destruction of photographs which might immerse us in a past that we no longer wish to remember; or like the way in which each has trained his memory. The members of the group exchange what seems to them of supreme importance in life; it is a time of great personal enrichment. It soon becomes clear that the task of self-reconciliation is co-extensive with life and is not the affair of an isolated act or remark; further, it forms a necessary preliminary to recognition of others: "When it's at work in us, it spreads to others too. . . ." One important discussion was about past events and how they could become "one's own".

The kind of language used in the discussions is basically an expression of the experience to which each refers; the vocabulary is taken by each participant from his own familiar cultural sources. The student keen on Nietzsche uses a philosophical vocabulary; a political vocabulary comes naturally to the business man, aware of the need for the reform of the collective economy; a psychological vocabulary is used by the young mother at odds with her children and also by a young nursery school teacher interested in the free expression of her infants; an ordinary, everyday vocabulary comes, a little sheepishly, from a cabinet maker just back from a pilgrimage to Lourdes. There is no special vocabulary; each member of the group relies on his own cultural background for the expression of his particular concerns. It is always a secular vocabulary, and the experiences recalled are outside the religious sphere, being only those of a man trying to cope with the conflicts thrown up by life. An expression of the group mind clearly emerges, and each member obtains something from it; words are pregnant with the history that they have been used to relate. The key term is reconciliation. On the other hand, we must remember the original reason for this inquiry: "What has all this got to do with sin and penance? After all, it's called the 'sacrament of reconciliation'."

2. *Atrophy of Religious Language and Practice?*

The discussion did not begin with a Christian truth used to throw light on life; instead, an attempt was made to interpret a

line of human conduct the importance of which was acknowledged by all. This did not resolve the difficulty of religious language without meaning, but increased it to an intolerable degree.
In comparison with the importance of this human means of reconciliation, which affects the whole of life and is imperative as
only a difficult task of great value is absolutely imperative, the
few minutes spent in the confessional and somewhat pretentiously
termed the "sacrament of reconciliation" seem absolutely meaningless. In other words, the range of man's knowledge has been
extended together with his experience, and as a result of this
extension religious language is investigated to provide verification.
"How can anyone think that reconciliation can take place in two
minutes, or that a moment can, like magic, take the place of a
continuing and demanding effort? Months and years are needed
to bring to a successful conclusion the first rudiments of reconciliation with certain events of the past. Yet the Church tells us:
"Are you torn by interior conflict and division? Into the confessional with you, and two minutes later you'll be reconciled.
What are you waiting for?" This sort of thing used to be only
half unacceptable; now it's wholly so." Man's entire responsibility turns him away from the religious aspect of life; it is reconciliation *in his life* which is held in esteem. "How can one
compare the gradual endeavour of a man who for months is brave
enough to undertake what we have been talking about and the
conduct of a pious old woman who every fortnight, regular as
clockwork, takes her place in the passive queue of penitents outside the parish priest's confessional? Surely the Church's ideas are
absolutely unreasonable!"

But does this really represent the Church's essential ideas? Must
we look for something else beneath the dust and all the rule of
thumb methods? *Where* are the sacraments? *When* is a man reconciled? Can the sacrament be effective in an instant when what
is in closest affinity with it constitutes an enduring reality, co-
extensive with the whole of life? At first sight, the sacrament
concerns our reconciliation with God, and what we have been
considering concerns our reconciliation with ourselves. Are these
the same thing? Haven't we confused psychology with salvation? But if salvation has nothing whatever to do with

psychology, sociology, politics or professional matters, what exactly does it cover? Or is it just empty words?

The many questions raised would require treatment at length to show the path taken by the group's inquiry. I must confine myself to one aspect of the matter which seems particularly important—though I must ask the more theologically minded to be patient with their questions.

This anthropological study of reconciliation emphasized a somewhat unexpected aspect of the sacrament of penance. If the discussion had been based on the religious reality this aspect would probably not have been considered. It was shown that reconciliation is far more a victory over a wrong idea of limitations than over the guilt resulting from sin. We parish priests avoid the difficulty too easily by saying that people no longer have any sense of sin. But some explanation is required at this point.

3. Man's Powerlessness in Self-realization and the Recognition of Limitations

Apparently the group's more or less conscious intention was to give new human significance to a liturgical act. The group investigated what in secular life showed some affinity with what was supposed to happen in church. It emerged that the greatest obstacle to reconciliation was man's inability to realize himself completely, to achieve his aspirations to the full and to live at the level where he can say, "I am really myself", without reservations. How can a man live at peace with himself when he is thinking of "being himself" in such absolutist terms? It is the same with the mother who, when her elder children need a certain privacy to be able to breathe, wants complete openness between all members of the family. There is the business man who feels bound to absolute integrity in his profession when it is clear that he cannot achieve one end without sacrificing others. There is the young student who, in the name of the loftiest moral aspirations, feels bound to realize to the full all that he is capable of, yet soon discovers that it is impossible to do so and indeed that the universe of values is not coherent, that you cannot choose without excluding, that every option has its contrary. In all this there is no trace of sin, but only a sort of natural rigidity which is merely the symptom of our limitations. As long as we retain an absolutist image of ourselves, it is hard to see how we can live with such limitations without considerable reservations. This is the situation clearly analysed by Ricoeur: "Who can achieve self-realization without exclusion not only of possibilities but of realities and existences and, as a result, without destruction ... ? *I* raise what is inescapable in myself and outside myself by the development of my own existence. It is then no longer a sin in the ethical sense of a transgression of the law but in the existential sense: to become oneself means failure to achieve full realization, which nevertheless remains the end, the dream, the horizon, which the idea of happiness shows. Because destiny belongs to freedom as the unchosen part of all our options, it must be experienced as sin. ..."[1]

The group's reflection developed along these lines: we must come to terms with our limitations. There can be no question of our regarding this as sin, any more than we can avoid re-thinking our human state; it cannot be taken as a matter of course.

But how can this task, which is of such importance in a man's existence, find no expression for a Christian in the sacrament of penance? Apparently, in the sacrament as it is ordinarily administered, or in services of penance, there is no trace to be found of this daily task by which a man comes to terms with his human state. Therefore the group began to investigate the theological reality of the sacrament in order to discover whether what is fundamental in religion is rooted in what is fundamental in life. In this context, I believe, a "forgotten truth" of the sacrament of penance was rediscovered.

It is no small matter to give up living according to an autocratic pattern; to admit, that is, not only verbally but even in the form of the most fundamental actions, that one is not an absolute centre of attribution, reference and judgment (in judging, everyone acts God", Pascal remarked). "As having nothing, and yet possessing all things", said St Paul.

When a man undertakes this task and has broken away from fascination with the divine, he is on the verge of a religious attitude that—in one sense—is wholly transcendent. Isn't the statement "I am not God" the first step to thanksgiving? By giving up

[1] P. Ricoeur, *Finitude et culpabilité*, II (1960), pp. 290-1.

a place that is not his own, man gives back to God what is God's, and thanks him for being what he is. For man, acknowledgment of his limitations is correlative with thanksgiving. And when acceptance of this limitation is experienced in the joy of truth refound, thanksgiving becomes a celebration. Every sacrament is this in the first place.

All this, it seems to me, reverses the meaning of the question, "How are we to express the faith for people today in their own language?" After all, this language belongs to them. Acceptance of a kind of feedback from culture to the faith seems to me an essential requirement for the Church at the present time. The broadening of man's self-awareness seems to offer a great opportunity of discovering or rediscovering the rich meanings in the truths of Christian faith. But the "centres" which produce them must be allowed to speak. This, I believe, is the catechist's primary task at the present time.

II. Life and Language as Experienced by a Group

Continuing my investigation of the language experience, I encountered a further set of questions in connection with the life of a group. It is probably a constant temptation to reduce this life of a catechetical group to the intellectual and spiritual content of its remarks, and to assess it in accordance with the accuracy and clarity of its statements. A catechist will soon discover that reality is very different.

1. *Logic of Content and Logic of Relation*

A discussion follows, of course, the rule of the logic of content, but not solely. By "logic of content" is meant the ordering of ideas according to a rational series of the different aspects of a subject, which ordering results from the subject itself. There is a logic of content; but there is also a logic of relation. By this I mean the series of attitudes in which one is caused by the other. For example, by the logic of relation, frustration provokes aggression and difference causes reserve—at the personal or ideological level. By the logic of relation, too, a person grasps an idea or a subject not for its intrinsic meaning but for the function that it is to perform. *Function* and *meaning* must be carefully distinguished. This was brilliantly put by Valéry when he said: "Every word has several meanings, the most remarkable of which is certainly the reason causing the word to be uttered. Hence *quoniam nominor leo* does not mean 'for I am called lion' but rather, 'I am a rule of grammar'." The creed said at Sunday Mass has a meaning which is defined by (the actual terms of) the statements made; it also possesses another meaning which, in the terminology used here, is called a "function" and which can be this, for example, in order to reassure those professing the same faith of the unity and coherence of their group. Obviously it is possible for the meaning to have no importance if the function, the sole determining factor, can be assured by any other meaning. When the meanings are interchangeable without effecting any modification in the group, it is probable that the group is following only the logic of relation. It has often been pointed out that many Christians would gladly exchange the dogma of the resurrection of the body for certainty of some sort regarding the immortality of the soul. This it would seem is because the same function of reassuring man regarding his future is ensured by both cases.

I think that explicit language always contains additional implications, and that in challenging apparently simple meanings, without knowing one does so or desiring to do so, one sometimes touches the need for security and the balance of the group which had found in these meanings support and peace. The violence of the reactions in comparison with the trivial nature of the criticism aimed at the meaning can be really astonishing. It is far more understandable if it is seen in reference to the function with which the meaning is imbued and which as a result is deprived of full support. What was thought to be an attack on the meaning is also one on the function, and only the disproportionate reaction provokes the thought that something else is at stake. A catechist cannot ignore this "something else"; he is aware that complete language is made up of this continual interaction between the logic of content and the logic of relations, but he often considers that the ideal would be to reduce this complex dialectics to the "objectivity" of the logic of content. I believe that this would be a still greater error and that the only possibility for the catechist is to recognize this complexity of the language of experience, in which "what is said" is continually made up of "what happens".

2. *Overcoming the Obstacle of an Established Language*

What is the relevance of remarks like those above? In the first place, they serve to direct our attention to the fact that *relation is also a form of expression* and that perhaps the most valuable attainments of a group come to it in this way and only in this way. The terms of religion are closely woven into the very fabric of relationship; undeniably, therefore, the key ideas and basic attitude of faith are pre-formed in the inter-human relationship, and cannot remain unchanged when this relationship itself is changed. All the contradictions retained between "what is said" and "what happens" in a group could introduce into its language a distortion from which all would suffer without perhaps being able to discern its cause. On the other hand, a durable connection between content and relation would give a group an entirely new and surprising possibility of interpretation.

Secondly, these considerations oblige us to seek other criteria when distinguishing between "good" and "bad" catechesis.

Thirdly, some interesting educational possibilities are revealed. Realization that language cannot be reduced to propositions opens a considerable field of action. I have often noticed that a group shows corresponding attitudes to the persons and to the subject-matter with which it is confronted. In a given group, as long as persons with their mutual differences are not accepted, there is every chance that the differences of texts will prove equally insurmountable. There can be no question of putting forward a plea in favour of the texts, or of seeking others of a less difficult or technical nature; it is necessary to cause the relationship to develop. If the group evolves, if the differences of persons, opinions and feelings can be disclosed and accepted as a permanent dimension of relationship, everything changes. The group no longer requires the texts to be in harmony with it; it grows tolerant to a language which is not its own; and it is able to understand that there is no language made for it save that which it makes itself on the basis of what is not itself. The obstacle of established language is surmounted, and the group language begins to emerge. The creative period has begun.

Translated by Lancelot Sheppard

PART II
STUDIES

PART II

Christiane Brusselmans

A Catechesis adapted
to the Present Age and the
Liturgical Initiation of Children

I. THE PROBLEM RAISED BY THE PRESENT CRISIS IN THE CHURCH

IT IS undeniable that the Church is at present undergoing immense changes which affect all sections of pastoral practice. Indeed these changes have even proved a major trial, for not merely institutions but faith itself is called in question. Men and institutions cannot escape these times of trial which are the sign of their internal dynamism and the source of all growth and development. What is important is the spirit in which the trial and the adaptations it entails are received. Fortunate the man, the society or the Church which accepts the trial not in a spirit of resignation but of responsibility and constant and active adaptation. Painful though it may be, the crisis affecting the Church at present offers an opportunity for reflection on her nature, for the rediscovery of her methods and the reassessment of her institutions. If this trial is met with lucidity and courage it will be the starting-point for new adaptations and further progress in hastening the salvation of mankind immersed, as it is, in a history which moves increasingly faster and is becoming increasingly irreversible.

The constant need of adaptation to very different situations, mentalities and cultures requires of those taking part in various ways in the catechetical and liturgical mission of the Church a fundamental attitude of openness to the needs of the world and the mentality of contemporary man. This need, far from giving them a sense of security, seems, on the contrary, to cause profound disquiet among Christian parents, catechists, priests and bishops who together are responsible for the religious education of children.

Will those responsible for catechesis and liturgy in 1970 be psychologically and intellectually capable of constant adaptation to new needs? A positive answer to this question depends on the powers of adaptation of Christian parents and the catechists, but it depends still more on the powers of adaptation, lucidity and courage of the Church at large in which they carry out their mission. There precisely difficulties occur. It is the problem of the position of the laity (for example, the parents in this case) in the Church: the extent of creativity and initiative afforded, the sense of individual and collective responsibility, decentralization of the machinery for taking decisions in the Church, a sense of challenge, and so on. But this theme—of importance for the reform of the Church—cannot be dealt with here, though the various questions it raises ought to be listed. Here I want to consider the nature, methods and institutions of catechesis and liturgy.

II. On the Nature of Catechesis and Liturgy

The nature of catechesis and liturgy comprises two fundamental requirements: the first consists in being faithful to their object, that is, to the revelation fully manifested and accomplished in Jesus Christ; the second consists in being faithful to the subject of catechesis and liturgy, that is, to man endeavouring to discover the meaning of his existence and, in the light of the word of God, finding an answer to the questions he raises. It is still necessary for contemporary man to be able to hear, understand and receive the word of God and for it to be lived, spoken or celebrated.

Both catechetical and liturgical experience prove that it is difficult to remain faithful to this twofold requirement. How in fact are we to show modern man, in a language and signs that he can grasp and understand, the integrity of revelation without at the same time depriving it of its transcendent character? For that character is peculiarly the property of the word of God and we have to avoid its being reduced to a mere human idea.

The difficulty consists in this: either we at once adopt a

position in the light of faith and so run the risk of remaining a stranger to the world of man; or else we make our starting-point what is of direct concern to man, and run the risk of remaining at that stage and never going beyond a certain humanism. We adopt a position either from God's side or man's side while what we have to do is to go beyond the two poles of the antinomy in order to unite them. Does the death of God result in the coming of man, or the death of man in the advent of God?

Consideration of the nature of catechesis and liturgy leads quite naturally to consideration of the nature of man. Reflection on every human action raises the problem of God and transcendence.

The man who reflects on his action and thought becomes aware that the reality of being in which he shares is not complete within the human or worldly context but that this reality lies open, finally, to transcendence, that is, to God. Our existence always goes far beyond our plans. "The human problem", wrote Fr Ricoeur, "is always that of man's borders and so on a last analysis of transcendence."

We can see that very few Christians consult revelation regarding these fundamental questions on man and his destiny. Since they are accustomed to a more dogmatic and less existential presentation of revelation they reflect on the mystery of God in itself. As a result, in any theological reflection that is made for man and on the basis of human existence they see an intolerable reduction of transcendence. And so they fear that God is denied for the sake of the glorification of man. Their concern is ill-founded. Actually the end of catechesis and liturgy is not to separate God from man but, on the contrary, to bring them into relationship with one another. And to do this contemporary catechesis will be more existential than dogmatic. It will be based on experiences and fundamental questions about the human state on which it will throw light by the word of God. Has life a meaning and has man a destiny? In addition to individual destiny what is the meaning of the immense surge of life, and of history? Whither tend the generations, cultures, civilizations and religions? All these questions are summed up in a single one: what is the meaning of the life and death of man? What answer does the mystery of Jesus give to this question?

On the basis of these experiences and reflections on human

existence the proclamation of salvation will consist in making a quality of transcendence break in upon human realities. For our contemporaries a faith in God which was not the final meaning of the most important human realities would be nothing at all. For the human world is the place for the irruption of salvation. It is there that we must seek Jesus Christ; there, too, he must be revealed. In this process there is no reduction of transcendence, though it would be better to use the term "transcendence of interiority" (Jean Le Du).

If it is true that God made man in his own image and likeness it is hardly surprising that man should be fitted for and tends to trancendence. God's answer to man's hope is to be found incarnate in Jesus Christ, the Son of God made man, so that man might become God. Man will discover the full meaning of the mystery of his existence only in Jesus Christ. It is for this reason that all anthropocentric catechesis is *ipso facto* christocentric, and vice versa.

A more thorough appreciation of the mystery of the Incarnation is necessary to remove the misunderstandings which offend Christians brought up in a way of theological thought, catechetical methods and language of a very different kind. Some, accustomed to a dogmatic approach, meditate on the mystery of God, "in himself"; they seem to have no place for a Christian anthropology. Others, trained in an anthropological tradition, approach the revelation of the salvation of God in Jesus Christ through their consideration of human existence.

III. ADAPTATION TO NEW METHODS

The adoption of new methods in the communication of the word of God requires that the traditional methods should first be called in question.

Down the centuries the Church has made use of very varied catechetical methods and terminology. In recent years dogmatic terminology and method have been given up as being too abstract and intellectual. Their place was taken by a biblical method and terminology considered more human and concrete. A certain amount of disappointment had to be overcome before it was realized that culturally the Bible is very far removed from the contemporary mentality. Its thought categories, its language and images often add to the difficulties of understanding for someone born in the age of computers and space travel. A return was then made to the liturgical method, but here again its language, rites and symbols are also regarded as foreign and ill-adapted to modern man.

The inherent limitations of any language or method, whether it is the doctrinal, biblical or liturgical method, has led catechists and liturgists to look for a new one—the anthropological. They endeavour to reveal transcendence indirectly through a human language based on experiences and values as lived by man today. In other words, catechesis and liturgy strive to discover the "signs of the times" enabling them to reveal transcendence in human realities. The principal question that the catechist has to answer is the following: what meaning can revelation have for man whose deepest aspiration is the full development of life? Transmission of the word of God in an anthropological context requires not only the elaboration and application of a new catechetical method but also alert self-criticism. The anthropological method applied to catechesis is only at its first very faltering stages.

It is inevitable of course that this method may lead to blunders; not without reason do some take fright nowadays when they find transcendence removed from catechesis and the liturgy. To discover this it is enough to read certain catechetical texts carefully, to listen to some homilies or take part in certain up-to-date liturgies, although, of course, it is the exception that proves the rule. It is by no means my intention to blame new tendencies and methods but to offer a critical appraisal of their action for a better application of these methods for the transmission of the faith.

IV. A Permanent Deepening of Faith

Those responsible for the religious education of children will notice that as well as adaptation to a new form of presentation, both of language and method, the problem is raised of a permanent deepening of the faith of the adult Christian. Parents and catechists are driven by the children to question themselves on the meaning of revelation in their own lives. When catechesis of children takes place with the active collaboration of the parents it becomes obvious that most urgent of all at the present time is the establishment of an adult catechesis.

As a matter of fact what appears principally to be lacking in adult Christians today is a firm doctrinal foundation enabling them to discover the fundamentals of Christian belief. For this reason false problems, usually dealing with points peripheral to Christianity (such as indulgences, the Inquisition, limbo, matters of religious practice and superstition), must be left aside. Having said this, however, we must not minimize the theological difficulties encountered by the Christian at the present day, for theological debate is no longer a matter for professionals but has spread to the general public. It is no longer concerned with peripheral points but with doctrines central to the faith, whose traditional method of presentation is now called in question.

Here is a single example referring to the catechesis and the liturgical initiation of children to the Eucharist. At present the Eucharist constitutes one of the important points in theological discussion. It is situated at the very centre of the Church, as it is right at the heart of the Christian faith, for it is the sacrament of Christ continued and communicated in the world.

It is not surprising that questioning this doctrine should cause a number of believers pain and confusion. The questions raised are often at very different levels:

Why must we go to Mass every Sunday? What is the meaning of the actions, rites and prayers of the Mass? What is the sacrament of the real presence of Christ? What is the reason for this presence? What does it mean in my life? What are the modes of this presence? From what particular angle should it be explained to children? What sort of language shall we use? Frequently it is when children are being taught about the Eucharist that many adults first ask all these questions. Catechetical responsibility which, after years of eclipse, is now very properly restored to parents reveals them as very unprepared for the mission that is now theirs. Having remained with the knowledge that they themselves acquired as children in the catechism class, some would prefer to unload their responsibility on to others and take refuge in silence. Others will agree to undertake the task but will quickly discover that all the rather materialistic images and physico-chemical explanations remembered from their youth are meaningless and must be abandoned. As regards the Sunday obligation it will be shown that the Mass is a vital necessity for all Christians and that the responsibility for this moral obligation rests far more on the parents than on the child, who is incapable of reflection or action in freedom before God if his family circle does not support his sacramental life.

In addition, parents and those taught will discover that the angle from which the Eucharist is now first explained to children is also very different from that used formerly. Then the catechist was far more concerned to explain the exact mode of the "physical" presence of Christ; what seemed of importance was to explain how and when Christ is present on the altar, in the host, in the tabernacle. Nowadays, it is rather the meaning and the ends of the Eucharist that one tries to reveal. The principal question is the following: Why is Christ present among us and in us at Mass? What consequence has his presence in one's life, in the life of the community, in the life of the world? And whither does this presence lead man, humanity, the world?

It is certain that the initiation of children (and of their parents) to the Eucharist from a viewpoint which investigates the meaning of things, of human life, and of revelation, obliges Christians of every age to acquire a lasting theological formation.

V. Re-evaluation of Christian Institutions

Psychology and sociology show among other things the influence exerted by the sociological milieu on the development of the child's personality and of its religious behaviour. And so the religious education and the initiation of children to the sacraments (baptism, confirmation, Eucharist, penance) will have lasting effects only to the extent that they take place in close collaboration with the family milieu, the basic unit of all societies. For centuries, pastoral catechetics seems to have ignored this reality. Religious education and children's initiation to the sacraments took place principally within the framework of the Catholic school and the parish catechism class. Families had little or no share in this initiation. There were possibly some advantages of convenience in the centralization and rationalization of pastoral effort but this latter was offset by the spectacular way in which

the children more often than not gave up the practice of the sacraments on leaving the Catholic school or institution.

This massive abandonment of faith forces pastors and catechists
to emerge from the too restricted setting of certain traditional
institutions. It obliges them to rediscover the value of the Christian family as a fundamental institution of the Church. The whole
effort of pastoral catechetics in future must be turned towards the
family, for in this field everything still remains to be done: a pastoral relationship must be built up with the families; a form of
training for parent-catechists must be found; something must be
done about the provision of places in which to hold the catechesis
and liturgical initiation of children. Lastly, a new solution must
be found for the catechist's place of residence. This will provide a
presence and more effective help at family, housing estate or district level.

The evidence of those whose pastoral efforts have been turned
in this direction has shown that pastoral visits to families and the
close collaboration of parents in the catechesis and sacramental
initiation of the children, give these families an opportunity to
consider their commitment as Christians.

Many parents acknowledge that by taking part in preparing
their children for the sacraments they have been able to deepen
their faith and to participate more actively and with greater
knowledge in the liturgy.

For other parents who have been baptized but are ignorant of
the faith, this effort has proved to be the occasion of learning their
faith and of conversion to Christ. Lastly, for many non-practis-
ing families it has meant a way out of their difficulty and, thanks
to their children, a fresh starting-point in Christian life.

Translated by Lancelot Sheppard

Sylvester Wevitavidanelage

New Directions in Catechetics
in the Missions

WITHIN the past two or three decades, most of the Afro-Asian countries have emerged from colonial status to become independent nations pulsating with a new dynamism, seeking to assert their own identity, tracing back their roots to the cultural and religious traditions of the past. No doubt the Christianity brought to these countries by the colonizing agents had its own missionary success, but today it is beginning to realize the need for a different form of "presence" among men.

The Church in the missions is beginning to re-think her commitment to Christians and non-Christians in terms of a pluralist society, as proposed by Vatican II. In most Asian countries, the "Little Flock" is actually living amidst powerful spiritual forces of the major world-religions like Buddhism, Hinduism and Islam. Hence, now more than ever, the need is felt for the evolution of a form of catechesis orientated to help Christians not only to preserve their faith but also to "hand over their faith" to others as the fulfilment of their deepest religious aspirations.

I. FACING THE NEW CHALLENGES

Until recently, catechesis in many an Asian country, barring the instruction of adult converts, has been characterized by an exclusive concern with the child-in-the-school. Here, too, it has been a training more for a kind of "sacramentalization" rather than for an initiation into a progressive maturity in living one's faith meaningfully and dynamically. School-centred catechesis, however, is fast disappearing since the nationalization of denominational schools, as in Ceylon and Burma. A further setback has been, for a country like Ceylon, the abolition of Sunday as the day of rest. In such a situation the Church is called upon to set up new structures outside the school to work effectively for the Christian formation of the child and the adult. Catechesis, instead of being a school subject, leading to success in examinations, is more and more being understood as a life-formation process, an education in faith that helps one to live the dynamism and the mystique of Christianity in one milieu. The parish and the home are gradually replacing the school as focal points of religious formation. From a purely child-centred catechesis, the emphasis is being gradually shifted to youth and the adult; from the preoccupation with giving a deal of "information" about faith and morals, to greater care in the "formation" of the "believer", who will assume responsibility for his faith.

Hence in the evolution of catechesis in the missions, the following considerations seem to be influential today:

1. The "historical moment of Providence" clearly demands that our people must be led to a deeper commitment as "adorers in spirit and truth". While respecting the devotional and contemplative bias which our people have naturally imbibed, there is a need for a certain "demythologization", for a purification of their religion from the many superstitious elements indulged in the practice of religion.

2. The presentation of the message demands a new way of approach to God in a manner compatible with the religious concepts, patterns of thought, cultural symbols, and so on, of the peoples to be evangelized, rather than through Western categories and unfamiliar symbols and signs.

3. Catechesis should aim at forming the Christian to recognize the working of the Spirit in the very environment and events of their life, in the minds and hearts of people of other religions with whom they live; yet they are to remain convinced and committed to the unique faith they have received from the God of salvation they adore.

4. It is imperative that proper catechesis should help the individual Christian and the Christian community to go beyond an

egoistic, devotion-centred, protective, bargaining form of religion to a more dynamic, missionary-oriented, out-going and charity-biased religion of faith in the providence of God.

5. Catechesis should also help our faithful to realize that the privations, persecutions, sufferings and humiliations they are undergoing in the many Churches of Asia are a phenomenon necessary in the history of salvation in order to give birth to a more mature missionary Church of fellowship and witness.

6. Another important factor to be remembered in our catechesis in our fast-developing countries is the need to form our Christians to take the initiative and responsibility in their own development, and in the development of their communities (societies).

II. RENEWAL OF THE CONTENT OF CATECHESIS IN AN INCARNATIONAL THEOLOGY

Deeply conscious of the special role of the missionary Church in Asia, those committed to theological renewal are now calling for a development of the content of catechesis with reference to this particular mission. "Theology determines the content of catechesis; catechesis builds the thought-patterns, relationships and structures within any Christian grouping. We can evaluate the catechesis and theology in terms of the Church they generate."[1]

In presenting Christianity to people who already have a rich spiritual heritage, theology and catechesis must be re-oriented to give "the universal dimension of the reality of God, revealed in Jesus Christ. The deepest truths of Christianity have all mankind as their participants and beneficiaries, whether they are aware of it or not. God is the creator and father of all; Christ is the lord of history and the redeemer of mankind, and the Holy Spirit works in every human heart from the first moment of creation. These truths can make Christians aware of the spiritual riches of all mankind, and make others see in Christianity the fulfilment of their highest aspirations."[2] These insights are being gradually put in the *forefront* of our theology and also in our catechesis.

[1] Cf. *Teaching All Nations*, a quarterly review on mission catechetics and liturgy, published by The East Asian Pastoral Institute, P.O. Box 1815, Manila, Philippines. Ref. Vol. IV, No. 3, p. 324.
[2] *Ibid.*

Alongside this preoccupation the practical orientations being given to catechesis have a further dimension. Ideas have been fermenting for some time in several Asian Churches as to how best they could develop a theology of the *plurality of religions* and the mission of the Church in this context.[3] Dialogue with any section of the people would necessarily mean a dialogue with a major religion, and hence serious thought is being given to the correction of attitudes towards the presence of these major world-religions, the basis or principles being the Incarnation itself. "Just as Christ was incarnated, Christianity should incarnate itself in these religions in everything except sin. . . ."[4]

Hence our catechesis should train our Christians to revise their attitudes and approaches along the following lines:

1. Appreciation and sincere acknowledgment of the deep spiritual values inherent in these religions, and consequently a sincere respect for their founders and religious leaders.

2. Association with them in the spiritual and social development of the country; solidarity in promoting basic human and ethical values like justice, honesty, temperance, chastity, self-abnegation, service, non-violence, patriotism, and so on, though the legitimizing reasons may be different.

3. Encouraging a deeper study of the doctrines of other religions, and more especially the study of religion as practised by the people, where Christian attitudes and values could easily be recognized and discovered. In other words, the approach towards Oriental religions should be characterized not merely by an intellectual and vertical dimension but also a practical and horizontal dimension.

4. Finally, catechesis will have to evolve a spiritual technique whereby the presence of the Christians will help the followers of other religions to recognize "Christ" as the only incarnation and culmination of revelation and intervention of God in human history, the universal, unequivocal and infallible sign being fraternal love born of the activity of the Spirit of Christ in men: "By this all men will know you are my disciples, if you have love for one another."[5]

[3] *Ibid.*, p. 321.   [4] *Ibid.*, p. 323.   [5] *Ibid.*

III. A Practical Experience

It is quite evident from the present trends that ever since the Bangkok Conference (Nov. 1962) on "Catechetics in the Missions", there has been a steady growth of the catechetical movement in most Asian countries. In more than eight countries, numerous dynamic centres (about 35) are promoting the catechetical renewal along the lines indicated above, the East Asian Pastoral Institute of Manila being the centre for the training of specialized personnel and experts. The "Asian Catechetical Study Week" at Manila (April 1967), in assessing the progress of the modern catechetical movement in the East, recognized the general awakening to an awareness in all countries of the challenge of the times in very concrete terms. The experiences of several countries gave evidence to this fact. A brief statement of the main aspects of the development of the catechetical apostolate in a country which has experienced some drastic changes in the political, educational and religious fields since independence might prove useful here. Starting from the inspiration received from the Bangkok Conference, Ceylon has developed its catechetical movement along the following lines:

1. Training of specialized personnel in the International Centres of Catechetics: "Lumen Vitae", Brussels; Institut Catholique de Paris; East Asian Pastoral Institute, Manila. (More than 15 people have qualified during the last five years for the six dioceses.)

2. The appointment of a National Catechetical Commission (1963), the Diocesan Commissions; organization of the National Catechetical Centre and Diocesan Centres.

3. Introduction of new trends in catechetics, both in content and method, with a definite kerygmatic orientation by:

—Complete revision of the school syllabus (grades I–XI) for the whole island.

—Introduction of a complete set of new catechism textbooks in the vernacular, being adaptations of the "On Our Way" series and the German Catechism.

—Preparation of a complete set of teachers' handbooks and other ancillary books for catechists in the vernaculars.

—Introduction of a programme for the training or the re-training of teachers (lay and religious), catechists and pastors through the help of educational centres like the National Pontifical Seminary, Catholic University College and the National Catechetical Centre.

4. Revision of structures, shifting the emphasis gradually from the school and child-centred catechesis to home and parish-centred catechesis, covering all members of the community (children and youth and adults) by:

—Organization of a special catechetical programme for youth with particular emphasis on an existential catechesis of situations.

—Inauguration of a marriage-preparation course and a parent-educator programme.

—Promoting a wider and more effective use of audio-visual aids and other mass media, and an attempt to train young people to appreciate values presented in these fields.

—Training of professional and volunteer catechists to help in the parishes, providing them with necessary equipment (lesson notes, etc.).

—Attempting to teach children and especially the adults in their own environments, by relating Christianity to their day-to-day life problems.

—Diffusion of catechetical literature, especially a home magazine catering for the catechetical needs of all age groups.

—Enlisting the support and co-operation of organized lay apostolate movements and mobilizing religious as catechists.

5. A special effort in promoting the study of the Scriptures with the co-operation of other Christian denominations and the Bible Societies, and a gradual training of pastors and catechists in the use of the power and inspiration of liturgy in the Christian formation of the community.

IV. Some Urgent Needs in Mission Catechesis

A keenly felt need in the progressive evolution of the catechetical apostolate in the missions is the production of original textbooks. The new catechism should not only bring up the main facts of the history of salvation, but should explain them according to the mentality of the people in each country: the contemplative-minded orientals who do not have high "intellectual" attainments think more by association, proverbs and comparisons with their daily problems of life.

On the other hand, such adaptation would be impossible without special research and study, which is being undertaken in several countries in Asia and Africa. This augurs well for the future of catechesis in the missions.

In areas which have not yet been evangelized, with the exception of countries like Taiwan and Japan, no serious attempt is being made to direct the apostolate towards unbelievers who are not positively interested in religion. This should normally be a major missionary concern and should be in the forefront of our pastoral programmes. Mention should also be made of the imperative need to present an undivided Christianity to non-Christians who are often scandalized by our own divisions. Hence the need for more ecumenical activity and a united effort to present Christ and his salvation to the unbeliever.

In my thinking, an effective programme of catechetical activity requires dynamic leadership and inspiration from pastors, at the highest level. "The catechetical renewal will be doomed to failure if we train only catechists and leave the clergy in the cold", observes a missionary. In fact, priests, religious and laity should meet together to organize their ideas and means of the apostolate in different but complementary systems, so as to help the children, adolescents and the adults to encounter God, discover his message and adhere to it with conviction and love.

Tjeu van den Berk

Language in the Dutch Catechism

THE FAITHFUL want catechetics to cast light on reality in its deepest dimension.[1] Here the use of language plays an essential part. One could even describe catechetics as the verbal expression of the ultimate meaning of our existence.

In this article I would like to make a few observations about the catechetical use of language in the Dutch Catechism.[2] These observations are simply meant to point to the various kinds of language used there.

Every kind of language, however, obviously already implies an interpretation of reality, so that in the way the Catechism uses language we can see the kind of reality it is concerned with. Lack of space makes it impossible to pursue these interpretations in themselves.

We can distinguish three kinds of language: the logical, the mythological and the mythical.

Logical language is concerned with empirical, factual reality as it is used by the exact sciences. It conveys objective information.

Mythological language is used when we talk about the human values of man's existence, about things that can no longer be expressed exactly, such as love and hatred, life and death, God and man. It is concerned with reality as experienced by man and with the mystery which this reality conceals.

[1] Cf. *Grondlijnen voor een vernieuwde schoolkatechese* (Nijmegen, 1964), p. 31.
[2] *A New Catechism. Catholic Faith for Adults* (London, 1967, Burns & Oates/Herder and Herder).

Mythical language no longer deals with human reality, either because it speaks about a world which is totally detached from it, or because it only partially reflects human reality and so becomes un-real.

I should like to show that the Dutch Catechism uses all these three kinds of language.

I. Mythological Language in the Dutch Catechism

A mere glance at the Catechism already reveals the use of this language. Part One is entitled "The Mystery of Existence". On p. 3 it says that "we, too, as Christians, are men with inquiring minds". And towards the end: "We would be glad to end this book by rounding off the subject nicely, by putting the last touches to the painting in the sanctuary, and saying: there is God. But it cannot be done this way. . . . Those who wish to live with God find that nothing is ever rounded off" (p. 501). It also talks about "humanity's groping quest for God" (p. 33). And on p. 238 we read: "Questioning, searching, groping, the human mind forms an idea of what the Other, the Transcendent, should be."

This is something that is almost wholly new in a "proclamation of the faith for adults".[3] It seems to me that the pages where this kind of language is used, "where arguments and definitions and dogmas are dropped",[4] are the finest in the Catechism, and that their value will endure.

II. Logical Language in the Catechism

Logical language imposes itself where we have to do with facts, objective information and exact sciences. Problems of a historical, physical and sociological kind must be recognized as such. These sciences establish facts. "Faith does not establish facts, but interprets them."[5] If we do not recognize these facts, observed by secular sciences, we no longer know what we are talking about when it comes to "interpretation".

[3] Cf. K. Fens, in *De Tijd*, 22 June 1968.
[4] H. Oosterhuis, *In het voorbijgaan* (2nd edn., Utrecht, 1968), p. 238.
[5] T. Sartory, *Herinterpretatie van het geloof* (Hilversum/Antwerp, 1966), p. 15.

When the Catechism uses this kind of language, it again opens up new and hopeful perspectives. It clearly shows that the conflict between faith and science was a false conflict. "Is faith surer than science? It has a certainty of a different sort" (p. 293). "What is true according to science cannot be contrary to faith" (p. 439). Particularly where the origin of life is concerned (pp. 9–12), evolution is firmly brought in. The consequent new image of the world is clearly set out. "Our view of the world is no longer static but dynamic. This means that the authentic enlightenment is to be sought not in the beginning but in the course of things and their culmination" (p. 263).

History, too, is frankly accepted. To give only one example: "What scientific history can say of Jesus' resurrection is this: that the disciples testified to it. No human eyes saw the actual resurrection itself. It escapes historical observation" (p. 178).

Precisely because of the understanding of reality given by these sciences, the authors emphasize the great lines of history, which mark the way in which the book was conceived. "The manifestation of God's glory took place in human history" (p. 22). "In Israel's eventful history and through the words she spoke as that history unfolded, God gave his unique revelation" (p. 51).

We notice this historical development when we glance at the Table of Contents. It is obvious that particularly the interpretation of Scripture has changed considerably in this Catechism, and the reason is precisely the application of the exact sciences (pp. 38–63 and 203–213).

Frequently the Catechism shows that this logical language has been properly understood. This is not only valuable but also new where catechisms are concerned.

III. Mythological Language in the Catechism

When somebody speaks with a certain amount of "depth" but does not start from our human reality, then his language is no longer mythological but mythical. This can happen in two ways: he either talks about a reality other than ours, or he can give an incomplete picture of our reality.

We only know our own reality

It has for a long time been typical of Christians to think in terms of two worlds: divine and earthly, sacred and profane, supernatural and natural, and so on. If we accept that God speaks to us through the very happening of our own reality, and that we can obviously not think in terms of a reality outside our own, we become extremely critical, uncomprehending or indifferent with regard to certain statements about a heaven, a God who intervenes, a God who becomes man, miracles and apparitions.

Let us look at some texts from the Dutch Catechism about Christ, chosen at random. It asks what God's word is for us and says that the Father gives us access to him in the Son of this earth who is at the same time the Son of the Father. "Through contact with the body of Jesus, once dead but raised to a new life, we have contact with the redeemed world, with the kingdom" (p. 167). "Jesus ransomed or redeemed us by his blood" (p. 281). "Jesus did what neither Buddha nor Mohammed nor Marx nor anyone else ever did, he rose from the dead" (p. 279). "But Jesus raises us from our impotence by the gift of his Spirit" (p. 277).

What does man today do with such a language? What is it talking about? However stylish this language, it does not truly communicate. What can the stories of the apparitions to the Apostles mean in this context? "Thus in his visible apparitions he instructed his disciples as regards his invisible presence" (p. 184). And what about the miracles? "The miracles narrated of Jesus have on the whole such original and characteristic traits that there is only one conclusion possible: that Jesus did in fact work miracles" (p. 108). And what about Christ's pre-existence before his birth? "Thus the New Testament proclaims that he who is born has already been at work in the world from the start" (p. 78).

Here we are no longer in touch with the *mythos* dimension of our existence, where we cannot do anything else but speak in images, mythologically. These things are asserted here too clearly, with the result that they say very little. Here we have to believe in statements[6] which are detached from our own life. It is difficult to escape the conviction that, according to these texts, there

[6] Cf. W. Luijpen, "De erwtensoep is klaar", in *Streven* (Feb. 1969), p. 511.

is still somewhere else a separate world and reality of faith apart from the reality of our everyday existence.

We must not dilute or diminish our own reality

On the whole the language of the Dutch Catechism is most satisfying. "Everything will be all right" might be its motto. And that may well be acceptable as long as the concrete reality of everyday does not get blurred. But it seems to me that this reality is sometimes presented in too rosy terms or partly ignored. It is, for instance, excellent that the idea of evolution is maintained at every level of man's life, but the authors too often forget that evolution does not only mean progress but the surmounting of critical and dramatic junctures in this progress. Too little attention has been paid to these critical junctures and no help is offered.

Let us take one example: work (pp. 426–30). According to the Catechism, work is both "hopeful" and a "burden". Through his labour, man shares in God's creation; it unites men, and gives Christians hope for eternity. But work is also "hard, boring, oppressive and kills the spirit". "Like all great human values it needs to be redeemed. The Christian message affirms that this redemption has been accomplished. It sees it in the three elements through which our creator and redeemer is acting: the growing mastery of resources, growing unity, and the resurrection of our Lord after passing through his passion" (p. 428).

I do not criticize the Catechism for not being aware of concrete reality, but because it provides no *concrete* answer and straightaway passes on to a world of beautiful values. It has no answer for the worker at the assembly-line, the unemployed, the tradesman in a world of injustice, and so on. The Catechism believes "that even a life which is humanly speaking a failure can possess personal value and joy and peace". It believes that "through calamity and disaster the Lord attained life for himself and for others" (p. 430).

Does this not smack of a religion which is the opium of the people? Where does the Catechism show real concern with man in his *concrete* political, economic or technological situation? Here the too romantic language shows a lack of a real sense of concrete reality. Man is not directly involved in eternal values but in concrete ones.[7]

IV. Conclusion

The Dutch Catechism limps. What else would one expect if we remember that it came out in 1966. It could go further when one sees that Rome has already accepted certain less important re-interpretations of dogma.

But what I have said should make it clear that one cannot divorce the use of language from orthodoxy. There is a Roman "reality" and a Roman "language". When the Catechism drifts into the first, it shows at once in the use of language.

It remains, however, in any case the book which has provided the first breakthrough and has opened many windows. It remains, however, in my opinion, only a first step in the right direction. And those who take the first step deserve more praise than those who take the second.

[7] T. Beemer, in *Getuigenis*, 199 (1967), n. 4.

Translated by Theo Westow

PART III
BULLETIN

Willem Bless

What are the Main Requirements for a New Catechism?

THE ANSWER to this question will obviously depend on the purpose for which a catechism is written. We are emerging from a centuries-old situation where a catechism was thought of as a book that presented the content of revelation in short and clear statements as a system of truths. The author or authors would no doubt be aware that they were dealing with truths of the faith, but nevertheless emphasized the "truths" so exclusively as to create the impression that man could be made to believe simply by proclaiming them. Christian society, or what passed for it, lived moreover in that satisfying possession of certainties headed by revelation.

All this is now a thing of the past. Or rather, our past understanding of the proclamation of the faith no longer fits in with the new understanding of man and his world. To force the present situation back into the old mould would not only be spiritual suicide but a violation of revelation, depriving it of its salt and vitality.

But the good news of the Lord Jesus Christ is still there, and still capable of making man's heart leap for joy.

When, writing from Holland, I tried to decide what a new catechism should look like in order to help people today to understand the good news, I came to the following conclusions. I had in mind primarily a catechism for adults because the proclamation of the faith is particularly important for them.

I. The Catechism must start from Human Experience

The first thing man needs today is to understand his own situation. And so a catechism must help man to see himself, his own questions and difficulties, his own suffering, and the human joy and encouragement he finds in what is good in our age.

Revelation must not be thrust upon him as an answer from another world, and therefore not really an answer at all. A man's experience is tied up with what everyone can see and observe.

When, in my sub-heading, I say that the catechism must start from human experience, I do not mean that as soon as we have analysed this we should "pass over" to revelation. On the contrary. Although revelation is a divine response to our situation, it comes to us as a human experience in the most profound sense of the word. Our human history is the history of salvation and of disaster. Revelation is either a genuine incarnation or it is nothing at all. We shall have made great progress if our modern proclamation of the faith takes our human situation with all the seriousness it demands. Only then will it offer us new possibilities of belief and the chance of discovering human happiness in it.

II. Proclamation must be based on this Human Experience

Although the old way of providing a catechism in the form of questions and answers seems an absurdity, a catechism is nevertheless as a whole a question and an answer. If someone were to preach and teach human experience in such a way that he failed to show how humanly God expresses and reveals himself, he would have a lot of questions on his hands but he would have no answers. He must no doubt proclaim the message, like St Paul, "welcome or unwelcome" (2 Tim. 4. 2), but the message will only mean something if he can convey this message of God's as a genuine answer, a genuine surprise in the midst of our human existence. To be faithfully understood this message does not need our human fears, but it *does* need space and freedom.

III. The Catechism must be a "Talking Together" in Faith

Here is the crux of the matter. A catechism must make it possible to talk together in faith. The teacher, or preacher, and those who are addressed, must not fall into two categories, the one speaking, the other listening. Both must look for the answers in common faith. Both must set out on the search together, and together they must discover that they will never find the absolutely compelling answer. Neither side can ever forget that both are caught up in the situation of "one who believes". The one who proclaims the faith must never treat his own faith or that of the Christian community as if it were a property. He is and remains just as much a believer as the one to whom he addresses the message. God's voice can only be heard in this context of faith.

There are no compelling answers that solve everything. Neither the Church nor tradition has an answer for all questions that is wholly clear and valid for all times.

Our speech must never contain an element of human compulsion, but always remain just an open invitation to believe. When we present the "marvellous deeds of God" as a system of truths (which is possible because they are indeed also truths), we run the risk of blocking this invitation to the faith.

The theologian uses his human reason when he studies revelation. This can be most useful to the catechist as long as he does not manipulate this science as a key with which to unlock the mystery of faith and seize hold of it, but only as an aid in his attempt to think and speak in faith. After all, every theologian has his own solution.

A sound catechism has to be theologically up to date, show knowledge of the answers theologians have tried to give to new questions, make a responsible selection, and use them in such a way that their importance for our belief is made clear. We must, however, remain within this context of belief, and every answer that is given must help us to broaden and enrich our belief.

Faith is a kind of surrender. It cannot be forced. It cannot even really be offered. We cannot go beyond an invitation. We are not in a position to manipulate the encounter between man and God; we can only create space, open up, prepare. Perhaps even that is too dogmatic. In the faith we can do no more than introduce a possible encounter. A catechism cannot decide for the reader but only create the conditions that make a decision possible.

Is this talking together in faith merely an exchange of uncertainties, and do we now live with these uncertainties where in the past we felt secure in our certainty? There is no plain Yes or No to this question. One who believes is certain and has certainty, but a certainty that is not founded in himself. It rests in him to whom he surrenders himself. Because our modern proclamation of the faith is far more concerned with maintaining this position of "belief", it stresses this searching and testing on the part of the believer or possible believer. In recent centuries the catechetical approach tended to emphasize revelation as "possession", certainty, thereby weakening the sense of belief. Today, that kind of belief is taken for granted and we are no longer interested in it. We are searching and groping for a far more authentic belief. To impose anything in this field is really to act without faith.

IV. A Dialogical Situation

The conclusion of what I have said so far would be that a new catechism ought to be dialogical rather than pedagogical. A pedagogical situation is practically inevitable in a didactic situation. Any good teacher knows more about his subject than his pupils, and it is his task to transmit this greater knowledge. That is why it is so easy to slip into a magisterial, a didactic attitude.

But belief is not, in its deepest nature, a situation of knowledge possessed and knowledge transmitted. It requires something else, and to this something else the dialogical situation is far better suited. And a pedagogical situation with regard to children and adolescents clearly cannot be the same as one for adults. A situation where people talk together, instead of one talking to the rest, where he who proclaims stands side by side with the one who is spoken to, where both sides listen together to what is conveyed by facts that speak for themselves, and try to discover together and to experience together—such a situation opens up far more opportunities and ways of believing together.

This new way of proclaiming the gospel is also postulated by modern man's need to see and recognize himself. He fights shy of an authority that treats him as incapable of thinking for himself, that thinks only in terms of structures and institutions, and ignores the necessary, specific contribution of every man as a person.

V. The Catechism must be Well Written

My last point for a sound new catechism is that it must be well written. It must be written in ordinary human language. It must be sensitive to the potential of language and through this show a wide range of ability in handling difficult themes.

Above all, it must be written in the context of "belief", in an atmosphere of mutual trust.

Translated by Theo Westow

Bernard Mangematin

Guiding Principles for Catechesis among the Yoruba of Nigeria

I. Limits of the Investigation

THREE ASPECTS of the present cultural situation of the Yoruba have been chosen, somewhat empirically perhaps, to be dealt with here. I did so because they appear to inspire certain reactions which I think are significant among the catechumens, influence their way of living the Gospel and will have to be taken into account in the preparation of any new catechism.

1. Contact of the Yoruba with "white" culture.

2. The change from an economy based on barter to one based on profit.

3. The presence of the forest.

I shall confine myself here to their effect on catechesis; I shall not attempt to prove and develop the cultural aspects of the situation determining these effects.

II. "Does Salvation come from the Whites?"

To the extent that the catechumens have understood monotheism as the dogma of the existence of an Almighty, the Father of all men (black and white), they have acknowledged with all their heart, "There is only one God". Some of them, moreover, believe that they have always held such a doctrine. Yet it seems that for most of them, the one God, that God of the gods, the Master of the world, did not occupy the place or receive the worship befitting his position as supreme God. It has even been said that he was the *Deus otiosus* or *Deus remotus*. Like the Jews of the exile who, when in contact with a civilization apparently far more advanced than their own, learned through it to pray to Yahweh no longer as the God of the tribe or as the national God, but as the Master of the world, the Being in whose hands rests the destiny of all nations, so too the Yoruba in contact with a foreign culture have been led to adopt a religious view of reality no longer on the village or tribal scale, but on the scale of the whole world. They have accepted a universal religion in so far as it helped them to understand and experience this impact of two cultures which upset so many of their traditions.

But how could belief in the one God, implying the death of the gods, be combined with belief in the godhead of Christ and his role as saviour in the lives of men? The doctrine of the Incarnation raises two questions for those under instruction. (a) Does not belief in Jesus Christ cause us to fall back again into idolatry and the worship of deified ancestors from which precisely Christianity with its proclamation of the one God claimed to rescue us? (a question often put by adherents of Islam). (b) If Jesus, a white, is put forward as the saviour of the world, does salvation therefore come from the whites? Did God love the whites more than the blacks? If the catechism does not answer this explicitly an answer will have to be found, for this is a question, and a vital question, concerning the very roots of the image that the Yoruba can have of himself and his race before others and before God.

Is an answer to the problem to be found in a Monophysite solution which sees in Jesus only his godhead, and ignores or passes over in silence the historical aspect of his work of salvation, tending more or less explicitly to give him the prerogatives of the Father, who thereby becomes again an abstract God, a *Deus remotus*? To hear the reflections of some Christians about Christ we might well think that many of them more or less explicitly adopt this solution and that actually they have not heard the preaching of the Word on the subject of the Incarnation.

Hence our catechesis will have to be very clear when it speaks of the mediating role of Christ the saviour, Christ "the sacrament of our encounter with God". It will have to take into account at one and the same time both what revelation has to say about the "jealous" God, as he is described in the first commandment, and

also what the Yoruba think of the power of the intermediaries
and of the apparent superiority of the whites. If the historical
role of the person of Christ is emphasized, it must not be forgotten that this is an aspect which is difficult to understand and
on which Europeans are too apt to insist, forgetting the "mystical"
role of Christ and his actual lordship over the world, as it is described—for example—in some of St Paul's epistles.

III. Money

It is unnecessary to have lived for very long in Africa to come
to the conclusion that, as in certain circles of the Western world,
a very clear distinction is made between what can be called "professional life" and "religious" life. This distinction may be regarded by some as progress, an antidote to the alienation brought
about by the encroaching realm of the sacred. They will criticize
severely some missionaries who do nothing about a catechesis of
earthly realities, appearing to be uninterested in "development"
and adapting themselves too easily to a mentality regarded as
primitive and out of date. Matters are far from being so simple
and clear-cut. From a catechetical point of view, a distinction
must first be made between what the "catechism" said about
money (hardly anything positive, since the division of subject-
matter into creed-sacraments-commandments was of little help in
preaching a Christian ethic) and what the missionaries did (in
many cases here among the Yoruba, for example, they built
schools before building churches). It would also be necessary to
distinguish between the signs given by the Church through her
representatives' actions and the way in which these signs have
been interpreted by Yoruba catechumens. Since in some cases
there may have been a kind of apparent contradiction between
what the missionaries preached when they spoke of poverty and
what they did in the eyes of the people, the latter had not, I
believe, a very clear idea of the social teaching of the Church.
Can it be said that even without any clear ideas their attitude in
ordinary life was in agreement with that of the Gospel? What,
actually, is the value now of the witness borne by the catechumens
in the market place? If their religious life includes their social and
even economic life (as it did with their former religion) what

fresh meaning does their new religion give to their commercial activities, for example? Their old traditions made no mention of "profit" for then their economy was based on barter. The new religion seems either to ignore the problem or attempts to solve it in a way that is apparently contradictory. And so the contradictory reactions of the catechized are hardly to be wondered at. It must be observed that it is precisely where the profit system is gaining over the traditional system that the Christians, unable to find help either in their former religion or in the new one, tend to turn to a half-realized atheism or to superstitious practices which have nothing in common with the real spirit of faith or the genuine scientific spirit.

Without wishing to avoid the problem, should we not in our catechesis return to certain of the values of the former type of economy, especially those of a personalizing kind, and show on the other hand that an economy based too exclusively on profit and self-centred acquisition of goods (on having rather than being) lacks soul? Hence, in the catechism, something of Yoruba wisdom can again find expression. It is a form of wisdom which is far from being outmoded by an acquisitive economy.

IV. The Forest

Yahweh spoke to the Hebrews in the desert and their religious life has been stamped with its nomadic origins. The Yoruba encountered their gods in the forest. They were not abstract and silent gods, but gods, who, like the forest, spoke to them of life, of growth, of protection, of greatness and also of death and decomposition. The forest was a place which conditioned a certain way of praying and meeting. The celebrations of the mystery of life and of death quite naturally were danced in this cathedral of leaves in which everything told of decomposition and re-birth; here the drum beat out an introductory rhythm to the "spirits of the forest" and to the mystical sharing in the vital forces of the earth. The wooden and leaf mask symbolized the terror and fascination inspired by the many "souls" and "powers" dwelling in this luxuriant mid-protective, mid-hostile vegetation. The forest may have been cut down, schools may have been built and roads opened to make way for the "secular city"; it has not been possible to tear out the roots, or smother its voice and its call, which makes itself heard the more insistently since it comes from the beginnings of time. There is of course no question of a return to the jungle, nor even of fighting against the inevitable process of secularization, just as there was no question for the Jews of returning to their nomadic way of life. Still, it is to be wondered whether the Yoruba really need all the sophisticated advice of catechetical experts who claim to have discovered the laws of group dynamism and participation; for long past the forest has taught the Yoruba to celebrate the paschal mystery of life and death in common. What it did not teach them is the mystery of divine mercy. The law of the jungle is the law of the strongest. It is not the intellectualism of a bookish catechesis that will take its place.

V. For the Future

In the three examples mentioned no attempt has been made to put forward immediate solutions to the problems raised. I have tried to show, however, given the somewhat special character of the catechetical problem here in Africa, that the solution must be governed by these local circumstances; they cannot be laid down by experts from catechetical schools abroad. The help that these experts can give, in addition, of course, to the living witness that they bear to the Gospel in union with their local Churches, will be to restore the confidence of Africans in the actual strength of their own traditions. "The mind", said Bergson, "is a power which can draw from itself more than it contains, return more than it receives, and give more than it possesses." The Spirit is at work among the Yoruba.

Translated by Lancelot Sheppard

Joseph B. Collins

Some Guidelines for a New American Catechism

I. "Catechism" in American Usage

FROM THE time when the Catholic religion first came to America, the chief source of doctrinal teaching for young and old, at home or in the schools, was the catechism. It was a booklet treating of Christian doctrine in question and answer form, graded for various age levels, modelled closely in language and form on the prevailing manuals of theology. It was unattractive, pedagogically unsound, and wholly innocent of the myriad elements that embellish the proclamation of the message of Christ. These texts poured off the presses in all countries and in all the religious denominations, Catholic and Protestant. This is the popular and until recently the universal meaning of "catechism".

Another kind of "catechism" is coming into common usage. It is a text devoted to the teaching of the Christian faith in narrative form, not in questions and answers, and one to be used as a general manual for teachers, older students, adults, etc. The model for this type of catechism is the famous Catechism of the Council of Trent which was published in 1565 for parish priests. The recent "Dutch Catechism (*The New Catechism*, to give it its proper title) comes to mind as an excellent example of the narrative type of manual. The present article on the new American catechism is concerned with the second type.

Work was begun on the preliminary production of a new American catechism in 1964. Archbishop Joseph McGucken, chairman of the Bishops' Committee for the Catechism, announced that a new catechetical text would be produced by the Confraternity of Christian Doctrine (= CCD) of the United States to replace the revised Baltimore Catechism (1931–1939) which was passing completely out of educational favour. The plan of the Bishops' Committee of the CCD was to await the close of the Second Vatican Council and publication of its documents before proceeding to complete the new catechism. During the intervening time, thought was given to production of a text that would embody the teachings of the Church according to the principles of modern catechetics. The project was approved by the S. Congregation of the Council in 1964. The National Centre of the CCD conducted a survey among bishops and scholars in the sacred sciences (including catechetical experts), which revealed in detail what kind of a catechism was desirable for the post-conciliar Church in the United States. The essential purpose of the new text was brought out by an overwhelming majority of replies, as reported by Bishop Greco, chairman of the Bishops' Committee of the CCD: "There was a decided preference for a narrative, biblical-liturgical type text, one that would be used only as a *source-book*, and not a textbook, for writers, teachers, pastors and priests engaged in the field of catechetics. The development of manuals and guides for teachers and parents as well as texts for children will be left to individual writers and experts in catechesis. The bishops and members of the advisory committee appointed to work on the new text strongly recommended that the new catechism or source-book should be largely narrative in form with a few questions for discussion after each chapter."

It is noteworthy that the new text would not be graded for various ages of learners, and would not lend itself to individual or group study, which was the way in which the graded texts of the Baltimore catechism had frequently been abused. Here was a book designed to offer a carefully formulated guide or directory incorporating the latest developments in theology, scripture, liturgy, ecumenism, catechetics and apostolic formation. Psychology, anthropology and sociology, as sciences allied to educational theology, would of necessity be included in the proposed text. There was from the beginning a fear among proponents of the new catechism that such an authoritative book on religion would bring about a "freezing" of theological growth, or that it would restrict the present fluidity of catechetical thinking. This objection was answered by a definite statement of the planning committee that the proposed text should be open-ended and flexible in structure, so as to permit new material to be added to the book from time to time as the editors saw fit. In other words, the new catechism will not be the last word in the area of catechetics; it will be published on an experimental basis and revised periodically.

II. Purposes of the New Catechism

After the close of Vatican II and during the ensuing *aggiornamento*, a meeting of more than 100 experts in theology, scripture, liturgy and catechetics was called in 1966 by the Bishops' Committee of the CCD, at which the main aims and structures of the proposed catechetical text were formally adopted.

The purpose of the proposed text is to be a basic source-book providing guidelines, first, for writers of books, manuals for teachers and parents, class texts, articles and reviews, visual aids, etc., in the field of educational theology. Secondly, the text will be of use to priests, spiritual directors, and in catechists' training programmes; and, lastly, it will be helpful in all kinds of adult education courses.

III. Doctrinal Structure of the New Catechism

The proposed catechetical source-book will have to present Catholic doctrine as a totality. It must make clear that God's self-revelation and self-giving require man's response. In other words, dogmatic and moral theology must be intimately linked, so that religion is seen as a true "I-Thou" dialogue between God and man. Obviously, in a work like this, the plan of God as it is unfolded in the Bible will provide the essential guidelines.

The various levels of maturity in the teaching of theologians should receive vital attention in this book. Truths which are known certainly to have been revealed by God must be clearly indicated so that writers of texts and catechetical leaders will know with assurance what truths form the very object of faith;

i.e., of unqualified intellectual assent. Other doctrines, it will point out, even though commonly and popularly held are still not certainly known to have been revealed by God. Such doctrines, still under discussion by theologians, should be unhesitatingly indicated so that no teacher of religion will present as a doctrine of faith what is still a matter of theological debate or discussion. Unless the source-book clearly points out the various levels of maturity in Catholic doctrine, a catechist may teach doctrines which the student will later have to unlearn. In so doing, the teacher prepares the way for later crises in faith which the adult Catholic would never have had to suffer if he had been properly instructed in the various levels of maturity in Christian teaching.

Much of the present-day Catholic tension and confusion on the part of many parents and adults is due to their inability to know just what to believe and practise during these times of great and rapid change. Blame also rests to some extent upon a false security which teachers of religion have built up in explaining a mere theological opinion as the infallible doctrine of the Church.

Many definite guidelines on the components of a new catechism come from the documents of Vatican II. These must be utilized. Their list would include almost a complete index of the documents of the Council. In previous Councils a polemic atmosphere or the specific requirements of a particular situation resulted in definitions which stressed only one aspect of a much fuller doctrine. The recent Council, however, reflects a calmer atmosphere and a positive purpose which gave rise to statements of doctrine and descriptive definitions of a pastoral character, seen in the full context of the Church's teaching. The definition of the primacy and infallibility of the Pope, for example, cannot be left entirely to Vatican Council I, but in a source-book must be integrated and correctly discussed within the total teaching on the hierarchical structure of the Church and the collegiality of the bishops as presented in Vatican II.

The new American catechism, although directed primarily to members of the Catholic faith, must be fully aware of ecumenism in its fullest dimensions. The scandal of disunion among Christians will not be removed by concentrating on the dangers of ecumenical encounter, but will be remedied only by positive programmes for reunion with total trust in the Holy Spirit and a willingness to take some ecumenical risks if necessary. The source-book should make available to the reader the essence of the ecu-menical teaching of Vatican II and contain diocesan guidelines on prayer services, sharing in common worship, and inter-communion.

IV. Pedagogical Considerations

Catechetical education, imitating the teaching of Jesus as re-counted in the gospels, sheds light on the basic experiences of children in their daily lives, i.e., the concrete realities of their existence, their interests, and the moral values they live by. Hence the catechetical guidelines will call attention to the so-called Life Experience approach or methodology. God's revelation comes to the child through the events of his everyday life. The word is gradually revealed to him through his own relationships, his communication with others, and his ability to take part in or to learn about the events and happenings of his everyday life. It is the task of the trained adult teacher, aware of the child's present situation, to relate in meaningful and relevant terms how the daily events of life have moral and religious significance. Thus the child is helped to experience the risen Christ in the realities of life. By reflecting on his own experience and the experience of people of faith as they live together in Christ, he comes to know a personal Christ through the same processes by which he knows himself and others. In brief, catechesis cannot depart from its role of testifying before people of all ages and all backgrounds to the faith of the people of God. It must, as it were, lead Christians towards the whole truth and the faith of the Church.

V. Multi-Media Ministry in Catechetics

The Vatican II Constitution *The Church in the Modern World* has had reverberations in all areas of Church life, especially re-ligious education. Psychology, anthropology, sociology have all contributed their particular insights to making catechetics more aware of the total dimension of the person catechized. Now comes another refinement: technology. With the lightning advance of scientific discoveries about the control of the environment, it is imperative that religious educators become knowledgeable about the significance of our technological, electronic era. Inquiries should centre upon: (1) What are the media that most influence man today? (2) How do they involve man in the formation of his values? (3) Can Christian educators produce the media that will communicate with man today?

Many publishers have swiftly responded to this new challenge. Most series of textbooks for religious education today include not only suggested lists of "visual aids"—a term which loses its significance in our "medium conscious" age—but kits for multi-media presentations. Films, tapes, records, sensory apparatus, lights, celebrations—all are now part of the religious class which hopes to explore more fully the environment of the person whom religious education, in accordance with the total pastoral mission of the Church, seeks to bring to fullness of life in Christ.

VI. The General Catechetical Directory (Rome) and New "Catechism"

Finalization of the projected American source-book on religious education awaits the publication of the General Catechetical Directory now in process of composition by a special commission of the S. Congregation of the Clergy. This General Directory was ordered by the Decree on the Pastoral Office of Bishops (n. 44) and mandated by a synodal committee in 1967; it would serve as a model for similar directories to be issued by the various bishops' conferences throughout the world. American catechetical experts were invited to participate in the formation of the General Directory. Many of the principles enunciated in this article are reflected in their contributions to this world-wide catechetical authority of the universal Church.

Franciszek Blachnicki

The New Polish Catechism

COMPARED with those in Western countries the catechetical renewal in Poland is belated. The main reason is that the dechristianization of the environment which usually leads to a crisis of faith among the younger generation (when left without the support of the Christian witness among adults) has proceeded there much more slowly than in the West. Therefore a revision of traditional catechetical methods has not been thought so urgent.

I. Centres of Catechetical Studies

For some years, several centres have been preparing a catechetical renewal based on the requirements of the present and the immediate future. Five such centres are worth mentioning:

1. The *Catechetical Commission of the Hierarchy*, which has for some years been working on a new catechetical programme and on new textbooks, particularly new catechisms that satisfy the theological and pedagogical demands of renewal; it operates through special sub-commissions, linked with several regional centres, under the direction of Auxiliary Bishop Jerzy Stroba.

2. The bi-monthly *Katecheta* (Poznań), edited by Dr Marian Finke since 1962, which provides information and discussion about the problems of catechetical renewal.

3. The *Jesuit work-group*, led by Dr Jan Charytanski, which concentrates on working out new programmes, textbooks

and methods for catechetics at the lower and middle levels, and also experiments with practical problems in catechetics.

4. The *Catechetical Section of the Academy for Catholic Theology* (ATK) in Warsaw, also under the direction of Dr Jan Charytanski, which conducts research and studies, particularly in the field of the catechetical treatment of initiation and the Eucharist.

5. The *Catechetical Section of the Institute for Pastoral Theology* in the Catholic University of Lublin, at present under the direction of the author, which deals particularly with the basic theological issues of catechetics (fundamental catechetics) and with psychological and sociological research in the catechetical situation which prevails in Poland.

The work of the first and third centres mentioned above resulted in 1968 in the publication of two new textbooks: the small *God with us* for the two first years of school, composed by Dr Charytanski and his work-group, and the *Catechism of the Catholic Religion* for the middle school (6th–8th forms).

The publication of these two textbooks was a decisive step forward in catechetical renewal in Poland.[1] The second of these deserves fuller discussion.

II. THE ORIGIN OF THE NEW CATECHISM

The two volumes of the *Catechism of the Catholic Religion*[2] constitute the first attempt at creating a consistent and comprehensive Polish catechism. It is the result of ten years' labour by a special Commission for the Catechism, set up by the Catechetical Commission of the Hierarchy. This Commission operated through three work-groups, in Warsaw, Poznań and Cracow-Tarnow. They started with an inquiry about the catechism, the result of which was published in *Katecheta* in 1960. The main authors were Auxiliary Bishop Dr P. Bednarczyk of Tarnow, Dr Charytanski of Warsaw and Dr J. Kotlarski of Poznań. The *Catechism* was published by a decree of the Episcopal Conference,

[1] Cf. F. Blachnicki, "Zdecydowany krok", in *Tygodnik Powszechny*, 27 (1969), about the catechism *God with us*.
[2] *Katechizm religii katolickiej* (Poznań, 1968, publ. Ksiegarnia św. Wojciecha).

after it had been approved by a Commission of five bishops, as the first attempt at a post-conciliar presentation of the substance of catechetics in Poland.

This new *Catechism* for the first time makes a determined attempt to get away from the pattern of the Deharb catechism, still used in Poland, and uses wholly new principles.[3] It is connected with the new catechetical development represented by the *Catholic Catechism of the German dioceses*, of 1955, and adopts that Catechism's theocentrism, christocentrism and general biblical and kerygmatic approach as its main concern. It has, however, taken advantage of the more recent criticism of the German *Catechism*, and so has been able to apply these basic principles more consistently. The Polish *Catechism* has completely abandoned the logical and static arrangement under the headings of faith, commandments and sacraments, and proceeds on the dynamic lines of salvation history. Its main sources are the Bible and the liturgy rather than the formulae of the magisterium and the dogmatic theology of scholasticism. It also makes much use of the documents of Vatican II.

III. Composition and Dynamic Approach of the New Catechism

The four parts of the Catechism are meant to correspond to the four last years (5, 6, 7 and 8) of the elementary school. The first part deals with God's deeds in the history of the Old Testament, but puts this in a christocentric perspective, as already indicated by the title of this section: "The Christ who will come."

The second section is entitled: "Christ yesterday and today" and treats of the "fullness of time" as manifested in Christ's life on earth and the way the glorified Lord works in the Church, particularly in the sacrament of order and the Eucharist.

The third section, "Christ lives and works in each of us", concentrates on the Christian life of the individual, against the background of the sacraments of baptism, confirmation, the anointing of the sick and penance.

[3] These principles were worked out in detail by J. Charytanski, in his article, "Założenia teologiczne i dydaktyczne nowego katechizmu", in *Katecheta*, 12 (1968), pp. 151–8, 195–200, 253–7.

The fourth part, "Christ lives and works in the people of God", deals with Christian life in the social context of the family (sacrament of marriage) and of the community at large.

There is a short final section, "Christ, the same for all eternity", which rounds off this survey of salvation history by referring to the eschatological perspective of universal fulfilment.

This arrangement is not only marked by its christocentrism but also by the adoption of a dialogical structure, since the first and second parts stress God's call whereas the third and fourth stress man's response.

IV. CHRISTOLOGICAL ORIENTATION OF SALVATION AND REVELATION HISTORY

God's call is put in the perspective of revelation and salvation in the first two sections of this catechism.

In accordance with the conciliar constitution *Dei Verbum*, the concept of revelation is made to encompass both God's saving deeds and the word that explains them. Revelation has therefore an existential and dialogical character. It is a call to man, effecting an inner change in him and demanding a response. Because of this the *Catechism* shows how each revealed truth is related to man's existence and formulates our response to it.

The position of the people of God is also taken into account—particularly God's people of the new covenant, the Church, where the revelation is constantly made actual as the call of God.

Lastly, the christocentric line is also maintained in the teaching on revelation, which was not yet the case in the teaching about God in the German catechism of 1955.

The Polish *Catechism* maintains this christocentric approach by constantly referring to the work of the glorified Lord through the Spirit in and through his Church, which is to lead all redeemed mankind to the Father.

Apart from the concept of revelation, the idea of salvation, understood as communion with God already here on earth, runs right through the *Catechism*. Through what is good God constantly overcomes the evil and sin which impede this communion, and through his love changes man's self-centredness.

This comes about through Christ, through whom salvation is

always a reality in the world, present in the Church, God's people of the new covenant. And so, at every step forward, the *Catechism* smoothly passes from christology to ecclesiology. This transition is provided by the presence of the glorified Christ and the way he has operated since the first Pentecost through the power of the Spirit in the Church. This work takes place principally in the liturgy, where the Paschal Mystery of Christ becomes present in the sacraments, especially in the Eucharist. Hence the *Catechism* provides a comprehensive and profound treatment of the eucharistic gathering, which is the effective sign of the mystery of the Church.

V. Christian Life in the World in the Spirit of the Gospel

The third and fourth sections of the *Catechism* treat of Christian life as a response to God's call in his revelation and the salvation he offers us.

Just as man receives this call only through Christ, so Christ is the only bearer of our response. Our response to God's call can only come about through our existential bond with Christ, which is forged by the sacraments.

And so Christ does not appear in the catechism merely as legislator but as the inner principle of Christian life. For this reason the Polish *Catechism*, in contrast to the German one, does not separate Christian moral teaching from the doctrine of the sacraments. It brings together under broad subject headings such problems as the sacrament of the anointing of the sick and the questions of suffering, illness and death, the sacrament of penance and the questions about turning away from and towards God, and so on. Morality is not seen so much from the point of view of the ten commandments as from that of the new life in Christ in the spirit of the Gospel.

In accordance with the Pastoral Constitution *Gaudium et Spes*, the *Catechism* deals broadly and intensively with the position and duties of the Christian in the world. It does so by pointing to the values contained in the order of creation, such as marital love, family, truth, property, life, culture, progress, people and the State, and international life, as values common to all mankind.

It couples this with teaching about the disorder created in the natural order by man, and the Christian's mission to renew creation through Christ, and to free it from self-centredness and other consequences of sin.

The *Catechism* ends with the doctrine of the second coming of Christ and the final victory of God's saving will. With this final reference to eschatological fulfilment, the *Catechism* once again stresses the dynamism of the marvellous co-operation between God and man in the realization of God's eternal plan of salvation in Christ.

VI. The Catechism allows for Variety in Methods

The form in which the Polish *Catechism* is cast is that of the teaching of doctrine. This does not mean, however, that it is tied, like the Munich method, to a formal catechetical approach. The authors rely rather on the use of various methods, according to the concrete content of the material. Where they deal with the word of God they suggest the use of study groups. It is hoped that in this way the pupils will learn to listen to and understand God's word as his personal and compelling call. This method is also proposed for the teaching of the liturgy, so that children get into the habit of seeing God's call and man's response in the liturgical symbol.

Where Christian life is concerned, the *Catechism* presupposes the active approach. The pupils must be trained to find their own solution to the problems of man's existence, first in the light of reason and at the natural level, and then in the light of revelation.

VII. The Polish Catechism is Provisional and Experimental

The first edition of the Polish comprehensive *Catechism* carries a note to the effect that it is not yet put forward as the definitive textbook for catechetics. It is meant to be experimental, to create a wider basis for discussion, and to induce a more definite confrontation with the problems involved.

It already seems certain that it needs to be revised from the didactic point of view, so that it can be more easily adapted to different situations in life. This is why experiments are taking place in various dioceses to examine various catechetical problems, but they are based on the *Catechism*. The researchers keep in touch with the three main authors. There are frequent discussions particularly concerned with the way the children in various situations take to the new catechism. This will lead to a new edition which will stress still more emphatically the existential impact of catechetics, particularly in the first two parts.

The value of the first edition lies above all in the enormous potential for fresh theological thinking and insights, in the spirit of renewed theology and the Second Vatican Council. This is why this *Catechism* is most valuable for catechists who need to reconsider the implications of their theological mentality, for most of them were trained in the spirit of traditional scholastic theology.

It would appear that any further development will be on the lines of didactical adaptation and improvement, not on that of new theological opinions. For the *Catechism* has taken the kind of line in theological renewal in depth which Polish Catholicism requires. For the moment the most urgent need of the Polish Church is a biblical, liturgical and theological renewal in the spirit of the documents of Vatican II.

The problems created for catechetics by the world of "the absent God", as they are mooted, for instance, by H. Halbfas in his controversial *Fundamentalkatechetik*, are not yet the most urgent problems for the catechetical situation in Poland. Our main preoccupation in the quest for a kind of catechetics that fits the present situation remains the substantially kerygmatic renewal of our own catechetics. This was the task which the new *Catechism* set itself so appropriately.

Translated by Theo Westow

Wolfgang Langer

The Development of the Bible Lesson in German Catechetics

THE Bible lesson first featured in German Catholic schools in
the eighteenth century, and its place on the Catholic schools'
syllabus has been assured ever since attendance at school became
obligatory. However, it was always regarded as secondary to
catechism instruction, which was seen as the central point from
which hung the whole of religious education. Doctrine was passed
on in the catechism lesson, not in the Bible lesson, the Bible being
regarded as a useful source of ancillary material, a pool of moral
and religious examples and precepts, a store of object-lessons that
supported catechism instruction by demonstrating the authenticity
of the truths of faith inculcated there. Additionally, selected passages were read from the Bible with the object of providing the
children with a serialized account of God's dealings with man.
These readings began with the creation accounts and ended with
the Acts of the Apostles.

This explains why since Johann Ignaz von Felbiger and Bern-
hard Overberg (1797), school Bibles were always called "Bible
Histories".[1] The separation of these Bible history lessons from
catechesis was made even more pronounced and invulnerable in
that the former was left to a teacher whereas the latter was
reserved to a priest.

---

[1] Even when later they came to be called *Kleine Schulbibel* and *Grosse
Schulbibel*, they retained the nature of story books in which the successful
narration of the selected events was more important than fidelity to the
original. Cf. H. Kreutzwald, *Zur Geschichte des biblischen Unterrichts
und zur Formgeschichte des biblischen Schulbuches* (Freiburg, 1957).

I. The Bible as Concrete Starting-point

In the catechetical reform movement that developed during the first few decades of this century and that led ultimately to the establishment of the "Munich Method", the Bible took on fresh catechetical significance, becoming the historical and concrete starting-point of classroom work. Insight into the faith and an understanding of its linguistic formulation was to be quarried and developed through studying biblical events. This step by step method, characterized by the progression from preliminary study to concept, was the basis of the lesson structure of the 1955 German Catechism.[2]

For example, the doctrine that "Jesus Christ is the Son of God and is true God" (Lesson 26) was developed and "demonstrated" from such sources as John 10. 22–38 (Jesus' argument with the Jews on the occasion of the Feast of the Dedication of the Temple), Matthew 3. 17 (God speaks at Jesus' baptism), and Matthew 26. 63 f. (Jesus' statements about himself before Caiphas and the scribes and elders).

Unlike its predecessors from the Déharbe era, this catechism could without hesitation be called "biblically orientated", and yet the way in which it used biblical texts would not be regarded as justifiable today, either theologically or didactically. Its unquestioning acceptance of a naïvely historical understanding of the gospels, and its interpretation of words torn out of context, though in keeping with traditional dogmatic theology, must be regarded as totally unacceptable in the light of modern scriptural exegesis. And its lesson structure—from concrete biblical event to abstract formulation of a truth of faith—was true neither to the nature of the biblical texts (reduction of content to a truth of faith) nor to the object of catechesis.

For a new approach to the Bible lesson to succeed it was first necessary to overcome the influence of dogmatic theology on the interpretation of Scripture, and the catechetically incorrect arrangement of biblical texts according to doctrines of faith. The basis of the lesson must be scientifically substantiated exegesis.

---

[2] *Kath. Katechismus der Bistümer Deutschlands* (1955); English translation, *A Catholic Catechism*.

Initially, then, it was a question of establishing the Bible lesson as something valuable in itself.

II. The Proclamation of Salvation—not "Bible History"

Fresh initiatives came from two sides: on the one hand from the kerygmatic renewal of the Church's approach to the preaching of the Word—which in Germany was largely due to the impact of the liturgical movement; and on the other hand from the Protestant religious educationists, who had subjected the hermeneutical principles behind the classroom interpretation of Scripture to critical examination ever since the onset of dialectical theology.

The new assessment of Scripture's role, its reading and interpretation in church services, the Catholic Bible Movement's success in arousing parish interest in Scripture study, and above all awareness of the efforts Protestants were making to renew their approach to the Bible lesson, have led since 1960 to a far-reaching and lively discussion about the function, object and methods of the Bible lesson in German Catholic schools.

More recent German school Bibles, above all *Reich Gottes* (English translation, *God Who Saves Us*), have shaken off all traces of the old Bible histories, and by offering the children proper translations of selected pericopes instead of childish versions of them, have made it possible to conduct a lesson on the basis of the text itself.[3] But even in the case of these books, the nature of the selection and its arrangement, and the occasional paraphrases and commentaries, show that a compromise has been attempted between the hermeneutical and the traditional historical Bible lesson.

The breakthrough didn't come until after the fruitful encounter with Protestant religious educational theory brought about by Bruno Dreher.[4] Through him Catholic attention was for the first time directed to important developments within the Protestant Bible lesson. As a result, Catholics were able to accept the Protestant approach that Dreher introduced to them, that was

[3] *Katholische Schulbibel* (Düsseldorf, 1957); *Reich Gottes* (Munich, 1960); *Die Geschichte unseres Heiles* (Einsiedeln, 1962).
[4] B. Dreher, *Die biblische Unterweisung im katholischen und evangelischen Religionsunterricht* (Freiburg, 1963)—completed in MS 1960!

inspired by Karl Barth and that stressed "proclamation". Readers of writers such as Gerhard Bohne, Leonhard Fendt, Kurt Frör, Ludwig Gengnagel, Theodor Heckel, Helmuth Kittel, Martin Rang,[5] and others, saw clearly that the Bible lesson should not consist merely of information about salvation history and that its purpose wasn't achieved by relating it at every point to the doctrinal teaching of the catechism. They saw that through intelligent interpretation of the original saving Word of Scripture, the Bible lesson itself could become a meaningful proclamation of salvation.

III. Understanding of Scripture as "Work on the Text"

While the importance of these considerations was being acknowledged by Catholics, a fresh development took place in the comparable Protestant field. Where formerly the purpose of the Bible lesson was believed to be proclamation of the gospel message, the preference now was to speak of "an encounter with the text leading to understanding" (Kurt Frör), "work on the text" (H. Stock), and so on.[6] The first principle of an independent Bible catechesis was always to approach it through the normative science of exegesis. The school Bible lesson must start from what the biblical writer actually intended to say. This means that not only must the lesson be based on what exegesis has shown to be normative, but also that exegetical methodology must continue to be applied thereafter, though naturally in a manner suited to the age and ability of the students.

When Hans Stock refers in his paper on this subject to "work on the text" he has in mind a series of lessons in which the students "with progressive intensity and in increasing detail study

[5] G. Bohne, *Das Wort Gottes und der Unterricht* (Berlin, 1929); L. Fendt, *Katechetik* (Berlin, 1934); K. Frör, *Der kirchliche Unterricht an der Volksschule*, 8 vols. (Munich, 1953 ff.); S. Gauger and H. Lutze, *Arbeitshilfe für die evangelische Unterweisung* (1951 ff.); L. Gengnagel, *Mein kirchlicher Lehrauftrag* (1952 ff.); Th. Heckel, *Zur Methodik des evangelischen Religionsunterrichts* (Munich, 1928); H. Kittel, *Vom Religionsunterricht zur evangelischen Unterweisung* (Hanover, 1949); M. Rang, *Handbuch für den biblischen Unterricht* (Tübingen, 1939).

[6] K. Frör, *Biblische Hermeneutik* (Munich, 1961); H. Stock, *Studien zur Auslegung der synoptischen Evangelien im Unterricht* (Gütersloh, 1959).

the textual language",[7] lessons which are concerned to facilitate "an historically and critically informed reading of the gospels". The ultimate object of such lessons is an understanding of the New Testament in the light of the historical period in which it came into being, and of the dialectical tension between the historical Jesus event and the proclamation of faith in Christ which determines the language of the gospels. In this way it is possible to generate "an approach to what is to be learned and explained that is characterized by resolute, critical openness".[8]

In this way the findings of form criticism and the synoptic structure of the gospels is put to didactic use and even become the basic framework along which the lesson progresses. Among Catholics, Hubertus Halbfas was the first to suggest that lessons should include a study of the synoptic problems in order to avoid and correct a naïve historical misunderstanding of the gospel narratives and to promote an awareness of their kerygmatic nature. What is learned from this type of critical examination itself serves as "a guide to the unfolding of the biblical message".[9] Difficulties in understanding, say, a Pentateuch pericope, on account of the number of hands responsible for its emergence, should not be explained away by dishonest attempts to harmonize the conflicts, but should be honestly faced and put to didactic use as a key to the progressive unfolding of the text.

Information about problems of this nature and instruction in how the Bible came to be written should be a partial but distinct objective of the Bible lesson.[10] All this is within the educational

---

[7] H. Stock, op. cit., pp. 24 and 27.

[8] H. Stock, article in E. Dinkler (ed.), Zeit und Geschichte (Tübingen, 1964), pp. 704 ff.

[9] H. Halbfas, Der Religionsunterricht (Düsseldorf, 1965), pp. 129–43. Followers of Halbfas on this point: cf. G. Stachel, Der Bibelunterricht (Einsiedeln, 1967), pp. 157–88, 197–9; W. Langer, Schriftauslegung im Unterricht (Einsiedeln, 1968), pp. 32–40. Recently two books specially prepared for synoptic comparisons have been published: Synopse. Zusammenschau biblischer Texte, ed. K. H. König and H. Bützler (Donauwörth, 1967); Patmos-Synopse, ed. Fr. J. Schierse (Düsseldorf, 1968).

[10] G. Otto, Handbuch des Religionsunterrichts (Hamburg, 1964); K. Wegenast, Jesus und die Evangelien (Gütersloh, 1965); id., Der biblische Unterricht zwischen Theologie und Didaktik (Gütersloh, 1965); J. Schreiber, Theologische Erkenntnis und unterrichtlicher Vollzug (Hamburg, 1966); H. Gross, Kleine Bibelkunde zum Alten Testament, and P.

scope of the *Gymnasium* (where the student can also benefit from disciplines learned in the interpretation of literary texts in other subjects).[11] But in the *Hauptschule* and *Realschule*, too, this approach—again, adjusted to age and ability—is a necessary feature of Bible catechesis (K. Wegenast). The principal objective will not simply be to overcome the sense of strangeness that biblical texts, concepts and images provoke, or the misunderstandings to which their literary form gives rise (e.g., by explanation and translation, or by a modern paraphrase of the original text); the real objective is to appreciate the unique linguistic characteristics of biblical speech forms, and to make use in the Bible lesson of the considerable didactic power they possess.

IV. Language and Pedagogy

Reacting against the popular approach to the Bible lesson, which was to squeeze the message out of a pericope's principal statement while ignoring its linguistic form,[12] Ingo Baldermann turned the content-form relationship into a pedagogic principle. He argues that every linguistic structure is itself a didactic phenomenon. In as far as the biblical writer chose a particular linguistic setting for his statement, he did so precisely because he believed that in that particular form he could speak his mind more clearly and more effectively than in any other Any attempt to separate the content of a text from its original form, in order to represent it in a different linguistic idiom, runs the risk of losing or altering the text's original meaning. The paraphrases of the traditional school Bibles, the "re-telling" or "re-writing" of biblical stories for children, and even the more respectable literary attempts to represent the Bible for modern readers and hearers, are good examples of this.[13]

Neuenzeit, *Kleine Bibelkunde zum Neuen Testament* (Munich, 1966/1967).

[11] Cf. some secondary school textbooks: H. J. Kraus–G. Schneider, *Gott kommt* (Neukirchen-Vluyn, 1966, 1969); W. Trutwin, *Gesetz und Propheten* (Düsseldorf, 1967); *id., Evangelium Jesu Christi* (Düsseldorf, 1969).

[12] Ingo Baldermann, *Biblische Didaktik* (Hamburg, 1963).

[13] Cf., e.g., *Die biblische Geschichte*, told by Stefan Andres (Munich-Zurich, 1965).

In view of the above, Baldermann goes on to say that the lesson must develop within the limits set by the form of a text, and that the teaching presented during it should be that inherent in the linguistic idiom of the text under discussion. For example, where the text is an epic one—the synoptic passion narratives, let us say—one must respect the "epic distance", which means that a search for motive, or dramatizing, is improper, for both destroy the narrator's original distance from the events he describes, whereas it is in this distance that the horror, and irrevocable nature, of the event, its significance and timeless validity, is expressed. A genuine concern with the history of the period must be geared to full respect for the norms of linguistic form, so that the understanding eventually achieved is that which the text suggests to the reader of itself.

Quite apart from the heavy demands all this makes on the Bible lesson, there is the fact that many of the Bible's literary forms are accessible to children either not at all or only with great difficulty (it was this of course that led to the equivocal adaptations of biblical history). Baldermann's suggested solution to this difficulty is that Bible texts be selected according to their various literary forms and allotted to the various age groups in such manner that the difficulties they present are within the comprehension of the groups considering them. On the basis of his own teaching experience he has himself established ways of pairing student age and text type, and these methods can be used in the classroom so as to effect a distribution of the biblical material appropriate to age and ability.[14]

Other Catholics have endorsed the didactic consequences of Baldermann's argumentation while expressing reservations about method. Hubertus Halbfas and Albert Hofer have paired off specific Old and New Testament texts with particular age and ability groups and in so doing have departed from the traditional sequence of biblical passages which emphasized a more or less chronological treatment of salvation history.[15]

[14] Ingo Baldermann, *Biblische Geschichte und kindliches Verstehen: Neue Sammlung*, 1 (1961), pp. 57–64; D. Steinwede and I. Baldermann *et al.*, *Arbeitsplan für den evangelischen Religionsunterricht an Volksschulen* (Göttingen, 1967).

[15] H. Halbfas, *op. cit.*, *passim*; A. Höfer, *Biblische Katechese* (Salzburg, 1966), *passim.*

V. Interpretation as Goal of Bible Study

The problem of compiling an adequate text selection leads directly to another area of difficulty. If, in general terms, the Bible lesson is to be "a sympathetic encounter with the text", then it is not only the texts that must be appropriate, but the lesson as a whole must be geared to the ability of the children. This last is not achieved through an explanation of what a biblical passage originally meant (commentary): one must also establish what the text means for people living here and now (interpretation). That which once moved other men to faith should in this way become similarly meaningful to the children in the classroom. The Word must be "made present" so that it can once again become the "effective Word". In short, the true object even of classroom work on the Bible is interpretation. That doesn't mean that the class must on each occasion cover the ground between the biblical text and contemporary man. The Word proclaimed by the apostles is now a part of living tradition which has developed over the years out of the Church's ceaseless teaching and which itself represents an uninterrupted account of how the Bible has been interpreted. The Bible lesson can never be simply an explanation of Scripture—though the importance of this as an independent process must not be diminished—but must always acknowledge its larger context, namely, the interpretation of tradition.

VI. Interpreting the Bible

Inevitably, modern man encounters a version of Christianity that is almost entirely predetermined by the influence of tradition. There is therefore not only the question of making sense of tradition in the light of its biblical origin (Bible lesson as explanation of Scripture), but also the question tradition itself poses. For Christian tradition contains in concrete form, and in a manner contemporary man can grasp, the religious dimension essential to man: ". . . an awareness of challenge, and of dependence upon a superior being".[16] This persistent questioning leads man to wonder what it is that makes him man. In as far as a young person's

---

[16] M. Stallmann, *Christentum und Schule* (Stuttgart, 1958), p. 191. Cf. also *id., Evangelischer Religionsunterricht* (Düsseldorf, 1968), p. 17.

concern with Christian tradition initiates this questioning process, he is faced with the decision as to whether he accepts tradition as the valid answer to the quest for meaning going on in his own life (and therefore confesses Jesus Christ), or whether, rejecting or distrusting tradition, he is to look for some other answer, or perhaps attempt one himself.

Classroom explanations of Scripture are therefore placed in a double context: on the one hand an historical account of biblical interpretation, in which interpretation appears as the normative origin of Christian tradition in all its manifestations (preaching, doctrine, art, liturgy, Church order, and so on), and on the other, the context of existential questioning within which the scriptural Word can be perceived as testimony to the "witnesses'" original experience of faith and to that extent as the one remaining answer to the questioning of the meaning of life.

VII. Fruitful Conflict of Kerygma and Dogma

The central problem in the relationship between Bible and tradition is the connection between kerygma and dogma. In Church teaching generally and particularly with regard to its official promulgation, tradition is crystallized in terms of the dominant situation at any given time. The historical documents relating to the development of doctrine testify to the ever-changing "representations" of the original message while at the same time acting as stimulus to further reflection and to a living and changing tradition. They still affect the contemporary language of Christian proclamation and the present shape of the Church as believing and confessing community, which in its turn can only be understood when recourse is had to tradition and its origins. Conversely, the development of dogma is for the Catholic Church the official account of the interpretation of biblical texts. This reciprocal relation, in which through interpretation kerygma progresses towards dogma, while dogma (as something historically conditioned and requiring interpretation and evolution) is always subject to kerygmatic surveillance, postulates for classroom work a "dialogical relationship" (Höfer) between the Bible and the teaching of the faith.

With this in mind, Höfer pairs off selected groups of Bible texts with particular doctrinal themes;[17] Halbfas urges the illuminating and critical confrontation of biblical, theological and official, ecclesiastical texts;[18] and I have myself developed a lesson in which the students are required to take an official and modern doctrinal statement and work backwards from it, through tradition, to the biblical texts that "justify" the belief under discussion;[19] and in other ways also religious education is now being encouraged to pursue biblical interpretation in connection with the teaching Church.[20] The unanimity on this point, in spite of differing views concerning how it should be applied in practice, should reduce suspicions of "catechetical exegeticism"[21] which have stuck to German developments on this front (criticism from outside Germany has been stronger than that from within).

VIII. CONFRONTATION OF BIBLE STUDY WITH THE EXPERIENCE OF LIFE AND REALITY

School Bible study could be yet more decisively preserved from the isolation of classroom work consisting solely of exegetical treatments of biblical texts if it is placed within the second of the two contexts mentioned above: that is, within the inclusive concept of a religious education lesson whose object is to render comprehensible the proclamation of salvation in Jesus Christ as a saving answer to man's ceaseless questions about the meaning of life and about his experience of reality.

Even for Bible catechesis that proceeds from Bible texts an

---

[17] A. Höfer, op. cit., 3 vols (Salzburg, 1966/67); id., Glaubensbuch. Bibel und Katechismus, 4 vols. (Graz-Vienna-Cologne), 1969.

[18] H. Halbfas, Fundamentalkatechetik (Düsseldorf, 1968), pp. 264-7 and 335 ff.

[19] W. Langer, op. cit., pp. 47-56; id., "Biblische und thematische Katechese", in H. Fischer (ed.), Katechese nach dem Rahmenplan (Donauwörth, 1968), pp. 73-86; id., "Die Auslegung der Tradition als Aufgabe des katholischen Religionunterrichts", in G. Otto–H. Stock, Schule und Kirche vor den Aufgaben der Erziehung, Theologia Practica. Sonderheft für Martin Stallmann (Hamburg, 1968), pp. 73-8.

[20] Cf. int. al., B. Dreher, "Katholische und evangelische Bibelkatechese", in Katechetische Blätter, 91 (1966), pp. 67-80; id., Introduction to Gott unser Heil (Freiburg-Basle-Vienna, 1967), pp. 40-3; G. Stachel, op. cit., pp. 105 f.

[21] W. Nastainczyk, "Katechetischer Exegetismus im Kommen oder Vergehen?", in Katechetischer Blätter, 94 (1969), pp. 56-63.

interpretation is necessary, one that is geared to reach the point at which lifeless words written on paper come alive to the hearer as words that concern him profoundly here and now. *That* is interpretation—translation, in the real sense of the word—as opposed to the mere explanation of an ancient text in terms of what its writer originally intended.

However, given the situation in which religious education now finds itself, it would seem to be of doubtful methodological value to start with the text (that is, with the reading or telling of a biblical story). Most students lack the necessary pedagogical motivation: the Bible as such is not of much interest to them; they are not waiting for someone to make this ancient book clear to them. But among certain age groups it is safe to presuppose some interest in many of the stories that describe dramatic events.

Existential catechesis begins with man as a creature who grows through experience of himself and of his changing environment; it begins with human intramundane existence which in many ways man experiences as a question. Only on reaching adulthood does this experience declare its depths and thereby the urgency of the consequent questions—but, when all is said and done, the Bible is ultimately for adults not children. But even the child quite quickly becomes aware of the insecurity of life; it experiences fear, injustice, absence of love, failure and disappointment; but also joy, security, goodness, consideration, patience and forgiveness—sometimes probably more genuinely and more directly than many an adult whose sensitivities have become dulled by habit and resignation. Thus, consciously or unconsciously, children too can experience life as a question, and they, too, can benefit from the answer of faith.

The children's own experiences often arise in the course of classroom work and these experiences, or things they've been told about, can form an instructive part of classroom discussions about the meaning of this or that. Problems of life can be introduced through excerpts from biographies, incidents from films, and through poetry. Halbfas maintains that the interpretation of poetry is itself "religious communication", the occasion of an experience of revelation, because in poems the "depths of reality" can be revealed. In his opinion, the religion lesson doesn't have to include actual Bible study, although he nevertheless supports the principle that the religion lesson is essentially a Bible lesson.[22] In contrast, for Bruno Dreher a basic form of inductive catechesis is the direct and polarized confrontation of a poetic text (especially a contemporary one) with a "corresponding" biblical text.[23]

IX. PROBLEM AND MEANING OF THE DEMAND FOR AN INDEPENDENT BIBLE CATECHESIS

One way or another the pathos of the demand for an independent Bible catechesis has departed from German religious educational theory. Its justification lay in attempts to liberate Bible teaching from historical misunderstanding and dogmatic exaggeration of the traditional conception. The function of biblical texts in the classroom needs to be circumscribed for it is not only a matter of providing historical information and ecclesiastical doctrine, but of an "elucidation of human existence" in the world of faith.

But the insights that have been achieved as regards the necessity of exegetical and hermeneutical substantiation, linguistic precision and the selection of texts according to age and ability, remain valid and decisive.[24] Only they will protect an "anthropologically" accented catechesis from neglect, or an arbitrary interpretation of Christian tradition.

[22] H. Halbfas, *Fundamentalkatechetik*, pp. 209–30.
[23] B. Dreher, "Induktive Katechese", in *Katechetischer Blätter*, 91 (1966), pp. 241–53; *id.*, "Induktion als Weg der Verkündigung", in G. Lange and W. Langer (eds.), *Via indirecta. Beiträge zur Vielstimmigkeit der christlichen Mitteilung* (Paderborn, 1969), pp. 255–65.
[24] Cf. my comprehensive account in my book *Kerygma und Katechese. Theologische und didaktische Neubegründungen des Bibelunterrichts* (Munich, 1966).

Translated by Mark Hollebone

Iris V. Cully

Problems of Bible Instruction in American Catechetical Literature

I. The Relationship between the Bible and the Christian Way of Life

THE BIBLE has been the basic instructional material within United States Protestantism since the rise of the Sunday School early in the nineteenth century. The Bible has never been taught in order that the story might be memorized, but has primarily been used as a guide to the Christian life. It was presumed that a Christian could be known by how he acted and that the Bible could tell him how to act. Few Protestant groups today hold to so simple a view, but a basic question faces educators whenever they develop a new curriculum: in what way does the Bible point to Christian living? Two possible approaches emerge. If one reads the Bible, will one find the answers? That is, does the Holy Spirit guide primarily through this source? Or does one begin the study with life itself and ask how the Bible speaks? These are popularly referred to as the "biblical" or the "experience-centred" approaches to religious learning.

"Christian living" needs also to be defined. To what extent is it personal or corporate? Will devout Christians improve social conditions through the personal integrity of their lives, or does the social setting of a community affect the possibilities for the growth of faith? Parents, aware of their own lack of biblical knowledge, and clergy, disturbed by the inability of congregations to respond to biblical allusions, emphasize the need for ways to teach biblical content, especially to the young. Professional educators frequently insist that there is little motivation for learning the content of the Bible unless this can be shown to have some meaning for the learner's life. No one expects a definitive solution to this problem. In a "free market" those responsible for education in a particular parish would make the choice which seemed to them most appropriate. But Protestant curricula are subsidized by individual denominations. Various pressures, including promotional materials, leadership training programmes, and specific units of study closely tied to the work and worship forms of a denomination, encourage the use of an official curriculum.

Three solutions are represented in current curriculum development. Naturally enough, these begin with the Bible, begin with life experience, or attempt to combine both.

II. First Solution: Begin with the Bible

The thesis is that a knowledge and understanding of the essentials of biblical history are necessary for the learner to know how to live as a Christian in his personal life and as a member of society. Becoming aware of how God made himself known through the history of his people, he will see himself in this line of succession and know that he also must cultivate a life of faithful obedience.

The primary example of such a curriculum is one which the Presbyterian Church in the U.S.A. is about to put into circulation. Teaching goals are stated operationally in terms of the development of five abilities, one of which is "the ability to interpret the Bible intelligently". The American psychologist-educator, Jerome S. Bruner, has stated the principle that "any idea or problem or body of knowledge can be presented in a form simple enough so that any particular learner can understand it in a recognizable form".[1] The Swiss psychologist, Jean Piaget, has described stages in cognitive development from concrete operational to abstract operational. A core curriculum is developed for learners between the ages of six and fifteen (in American

[1] Jerome S. Bruner, *Toward a Theory of Instruction* (Cambridge, Mass., 1964), p. 44.

terms from grades 1 through 10). In the concrete operational stage the child is introduced to stories about biblical people (grades 1–2); he then studies four key periods in the biblical experience: Exodus–Covenant, kingdom, life of Christ, and the formation of the Church (grades 3–4); he concludes with a two-year survey of biblical history (grades 5–6). Assuming a basic knowledge of content, the curriculum moves into the abstract-operational stage of development by stressing the meaning of the material. Interpretative skills are learned in grades 7–9, where the structure of the Bible, its authority, and its interpretative method are studied. The interpretation in practice follows (grades 9–10): worship, ethics, theologizing. After this intensive grounding, young people and adults are encouraged to continue their studies in available elective courses.

This approach is grounded in Calvinist theology expressed in contemporary forms of orthodoxy. Highly respectful of biblical scholarship, the proponents of this method want Christians to know what the Bible says and means before they try to choose from among its writings what they think will apply to life. The methodology for conveying a content-centred curriculum is based on a pupil-workbook whose readings point constantly to the biblical text itself and have the kinds of exercises (quiz, sentence-completion) which will teach the learner how to read the text accurately. The emphasis in later workbooks is on learning how to interpret. Every classroom has a basic library consisting of biblical dictionaries, encyclopaedias, wordbooks and concordances to assist in these learning tasks. Charts, maps and time-lines help the pupil to grasp the geographical and chronological background. Filmstrips, records and films make the information more vivid.

Another type of biblical curriculum continues the nineteenth-century Sunday school method in modified form. A uniform lesson series outline is prepared by the National Council of the Churches of Christ; it is widely used by independent curriculum publishers who are patronized by Churches rejecting the less completely biblical materials of their main-line denominational educators. The outlines simply specify the topics and basic biblical passage for each Sunday in a six-year cycle. Old and New Testament materials may be alternated, but a whole book is studied in sequence and the basic writings are included in the cycle. The session outlines, interpretation and methodology are left to the curriculum developers. The larger denominations continue this as a service to congregations who cling to the long-familiar outline for biblical study but develop such lessons only for young people and adults. The independent publishers frequently try to avoid the theological implications of the Bible by using a moralistic and pietistic approach and interpreting the Bible as God's law for living. Stories of biblical people become examples for godly living. Understood in this way, any story can be used, even with young children; the overriding aim prevents the writer from being troubled by his distortions of the original meanings.

The basic methodology is to begin by reading the biblical text, re-tell it in story form, ask questions to fix the content in mind, illustrate with a parallel situation from personal experience, and then ask how the biblical story gives the answer for life. The basic method is that of question and answer (there is usually a "correct" answer), and the learner may be asked to provide simple illustrations.

The biblically based approach is rational. There is an assumption that when one knows what the Bible says, one will be moved to act accordingly. This may work for people with a deep religious orientation, but depends for its success on the learner's and teacher's acceptance of fundamental propositions.

III. Second Solution: the Combination Approach

Curriculum developers in some denominations believe that a contextual approach should be used but realize that they must write a curriculum acceptable to congregations which define religious education in terms of learning the Bible. These may start with experience-centred goals and unit outlines, but the development is in terms of biblical material.

The American Baptist Convention, together with the Disciples of Christ, has just completed the first year of a projected new curriculum. It is based on an elaborate series of objectives developed by sixteen denominations working co-operatively through

the National Council of Churches.[2] The three-year cycle themes
are: (1) knowing the living God; (2) responding to God's call to
live in Christ; (3) being the community of Christian love. The
place of the Bible is indicated by the principle of the "crossing-
point": "the intersection of the learner's persisting life concerns
with the dynamic of the gospel".[3] This is based on an extensive
list of Scripture references related to each theme. Most units of
study begin with a life situation, but in each year there will be
one completely biblical study. In grades 1-2 this material is taken
from the life and teachings of Jesus; in grades 3-4 it is "experi-
encing Advent-Christmas" (and a later Easter unit); in grades
5-6, a semester of Bible study and a similar course at the secondary school level. One of the three basic adult study courses is
biblical.

The Presbyterian Church in the U.S. (with the Moravian
Church and the Reformed Church of America) has developed a
curriculum with a two-year cycle alternating the themes of the
Bible and the Christian life. The biblical theme is described in
an adult study book entitled *The Mighty Acts of God*,[4] and there
are biblical story books for use at various age levels. The purpose
is to ground the learner in the biblical story as *anamnesis*, or remembered history. Other reading books and teaching units are
based on the experience of the learner; the Church is the basis of
a third approach. The methods for carrying out this purpose include story-telling, informal dramatizations, the use of visual aids,
and discussions which ask what the story says, and what it is saying for us. This is loosely referred to as an "existential" approach
to biblical study.

The Lutheran Church in America, in a curriculum completed
a few years ago, also tries to balance the elements of biblical
material and life experience. The learning theory indicates that
development should be from information to understanding, to
changed attitudes, and to action. But such changes are difficult to
evaluate, and in the written materials the understanding of

[2] *The Church's Educational Ministry: A Curriculum Plan* (St Louis,
1965), the work of the Cooperative Curriculum Project.
[3] Joseph D. Ban, *Education for Change* (Valley Forge, 1968), explaining
the bases for the curriculum, p. 10, p. 59 f.
[4] By Arnold B. Rhodes (Richmond, 1964).

biblical material becomes a strong component in both subject-matter and methods.

The United Methodist Church's curriculum (which is required reading in the largest single Protestant denomination in the U.S.A.) must be placed in this category. Methodist theology has usually been liberal with a strongly moral accent and emphasis on personal life witness. The Bible in Methodist teaching tends towards both moral command and moral example. It reflects a theology of grace with Pelagian overtones. A number of rural churches cling to a biblical curriculum. Although the membership in suburban churches is larger, denominational leaders have been loath to alienate the loyal rural constituencies, despite their own educational and theological training which urges them in the direction of an experience-centred curriculum. Some recent materials for use with young people at week-end conferences give leaders freedom to build on a wealth of perceptive materials in which the Bible speaks incisively to contemporary situations. This may herald the direction of the Sunday morning curriculum materials now in process of development.

IV. THIRD SOLUTION: EXPERIENCE-CENTRED

The basis for this kind of curriculum is the affirmation that the Christian faith is to be lived now, in particular personal and corporate situations. The Bible is a "resource" in the sense that it is the "lore" of the people of God, our story, and we need to know it in order to realize our roots. The Bible is also the human story. It presents the human situation (sin), points to God's redeeming work in Israel and through Christ, and gives evidence of his constant renewing power by the action of the Holy Spirit. The Bible is a living word as we hear God speak through its words, but a careful selection has to be made of the words appropriate for our time.

The United Church of Christ has the nearest approximation to such an experience-centred curriculum. The purpose is that the learner shall understand himself and see himself in relation to other people, to the created world, to the church community and to God. This is basically a psychological orientation. Biblical stories are chosen to enable the pupil to identify. Biblical passages are chosen which affirm God's presence or in which the prophets or apostles comment on situations in a way which would be pertinent for today. The wonder of man's place in God's creation is captured through some of the psalms. The earliest use of a full-scale biblical course is a study of the Gospel of Mark in grade 7 (age twelve). Further units on biblical material follow for the adolescent and adult levels.

This is an "existential" use of the Bible. The traditionalist would assert that the learner would never get the full picture of the biblical story, see its basic meaning, or grasp its essential unity. It could also be asserted that the criterion of choice would leave important areas of biblical material unnoticed, would over-emphasize some themes and ignore others. Proponents of the theory reply that only in this way can one motivate people to read the Bible and that biblical history arouses only antiquarian interest. The methodology is to explore the meaning of a biblical story or passage primarily as it might speak in a contemporary context. The child would be encouraged to draw a modern parallel to a biblical story, or to illustrate it in a modern setting. The United Church curriculum has a reading book for ten-year-olds on biblical archaeology. The framework is the visit of an American family to the "dig" at which the father is working. The ancient is made immediate and becomes a possible area for study because it represents a situation in which a contemporary family finds itself. The thrust of the discussion of a biblical passage would be less exegetical (What was the writer saying?) than expository (What can this say for us?).

The Episcopal Church's curriculum, popularly known as "The Seabury Series", centres on life issues. Whereas three strands are intertwined in the teacher's planning (life situation, Bible and the life of the Christian community) each course of study develops around a need of the learner. The nine-year-old, concerned about the rules of the game, needs to see the relationship of law and grace. The study book tells the biblical story from creation to covenant in the setting of a family who read and discuss it together in the light of their own lives. The seven-year-old, alert to the world of science, learns about man's place in God's world. Every teacher's manual contains resources for developing units of study, including one section outlining biblical materials that might be pertinent and giving suggestions for their use. Mark's Gospel is the basic biblical material for grade 6; it is suggested that the class spend the first few weeks reading and discussing the material (attractively printed in a special reading book), and then use it whenever it has bearing for situational units developed in the course of the year.

The basic method is discussion in small groups, but the meaning of the material is also explored through drawing and writing, role-playing, and the use of puppets. This curriculum is used in a framework that emphasizes the worshipping community, and in many parishes the family have attended morning worship together before separating into classes. Biblical materials from the liturgy play a part in the learning situation.

V. IMPLICATIONS

The question of the use of biblical material in a curriculum is never a matter of the quantity of biblical stories or passages used, nor even of the proportion of biblical to non-biblical material. The focus is on the goal to be achieved. Those who affirm the Bible to be the basic textbook for religious learning believe that the Christian must be well acquainted with the main outlines. The goal is to convince him of the persistence of God's purpose in the face of man's varying responses as the basis for the assurance of God's continuing work in his world and through his people. The purpose is also to help him, through precept and example, to continue this witness in his own life.

In experience-centred curricula, the goal sought is the strengthening and encouraging of the learner through the word of grace spoken to him in the experiences of biblical people. The teacher points back to the biblical record. Some would say that it is less threatening to see oneself in a person who lived long ago (as Jacob and Esau) than to be called upon to face ugly feelings against his own brother.[5] It could also be easier to stay in the historical mood and avoid the immediate situation. On the other hand, the experience-based curriculum lends itself to a non-religious ethicalism on the part of teachers who lack a theological

[5] Cf. Iris V. Cully, *Imparting the Word: The Bible in Christian Education* (Philadelphia, 1962), ch. 7, p. 106.

and biblical training. Unfortunately this is an inadequacy of many teachers in Protestant Sunday church schools where the system of voluntary, non-professional teachers is a principle staunchly defended as an expression of both witness and service. Such teaching ranges from simple lessons in morality to an intellectual discussion of ethics, but it would not be a teaching of the Christian faith unless it had a biblical foundation. A completely biblical teaching can be an escape from real problems. A completely life-centred teaching escapes being secular only when the teacher brings to it a deep knowledge and understanding of the Bible.

One problem, even in an experience-centred curriculum, is to introduce an emphasis on social concern comparable to that of personal development. The Bible is a book about a people who did not have the intensely individual outlook on life that characterizes the modern Western world. Yet we have managed to translate it into such terms. The corporate responsibility of families in Israel and of the whole people of Israel before God should enable us to bring biblical insights to bear more tellingly on the responsibility of Christian families, of the Church, and of so-called Christian peoples for the deep-seated problems of mankind. No curriculum shows evidence of sensing this parallel. We read about the disappearance of the ten tribes, the return from exile of Judah, and the scattering of the Church from Jerusalem, but are not led to draw implications for ourselves.

A persistently asked question is whether the modern person can identify with biblical people in spite of seeming psychological and sociological parallels. Are the sonorous phrases of the translation in the way? Are the traditional pictures which come to mind a stumbling-block? Do we need line-drawings, cartoons, abstract art, and multi-media presentations where the biblical and the contemporary overlap? Corita Kent's word-pictures bring startling immediacy when she parallels advertising slogans with well-worn biblical verses. Drama has been used as a method for involving the learner, but this requires more effort than the Sunday school can provide if the learner is to identify in a profound way with a biblical person. Films can do this when Christians are willing to become involved in the kind of secular interpretation to be found in Pasolini's *The Gospel According to St*

Matthew. Some religious people found that film offensive, but so did some who first participated in the story. An adult group could understand the compelling power of the crucified Christ over men more by reading Pär Lagervist's *Barabbas* than by studying a prepared textbook on the life of Christ. The professional artist can evoke the kind of deep emotional response which leads to confrontation and to commitment.

The problem of teaching the Bible to secular Christians is the problem of inducing those who do not read the Bible to do so. No device has had this effect. Church people are politely respectful of the subject, and they feel strongly that if children were taught the contents of the Bible, they would grow into biblically knowledgeable adults. The result is that adolescents think of the Bible as a children's book. The question is not squarely faced because many denominational officials still hold to the illusion that the insistence in the hinterlands upon having biblical materials, and the sales by non-denominational publishers of biblical curricula, indicate a widespread need. They do not. This protest comes from people with a residual biblical tradition. The crucial problem in American Protestantism is how to hold within the institutional Church the increasingly well-educated middle-class and working-class members whose very education and daily life incline them towards secularity and even scepticism.

A study of the Bible as the book of the acts of God, or as the drama of redemption, will not provide the answer. Americans are non-historical, glorying in the present. Moreover, biblical scholars have become aware that this particular way of affirming the unity of the Bible has ignored the Writings, has not sufficiently incorporated the prophetic tradition, and has omitted the Revelation, which is post-historical. Since curriculum development requires years from the planning stage to printed material, correction of this point of view will require time.

Protestant educators have yet to realize that the largest number of Bible hearers sit in the congregation on a Sunday morning. Much as we avoid facing it, this is the total exposure of most Protestants to the Bible. We would prefer the picture of the family Bible, of a daily devotional use of the Bible, or of parents reading Bible stories to their children. This simply does not happen; the long-cherished affirmation of Protestantism as based on a biblically-literate people does not exist today. The liturgy could become a base for a biblical curriculum. Some awareness of this is to be found in the present co-operative efforts at developing a two- or three-year lectionary cycle for Sunday readings. The stress on exegetical preaching in the recent past has been a well-placed effort to bring biblical words to bear on contemporary life. A few parishes have developed small groups meeting weekly to study a lectionary passage. The increase of vernacular renderings of the Scriptures is an attempt to get away from the numbing effect of the too-familiar. Making the most of this weekly exposure to the Scriptures may be the most effective source for bringing its word to adults. Generations of children have attended Protestant Sunday schools and grown up without any mature understanding of the Bible. Each twenty years a new curriculum promises to do an improved job, but nothing changes. The problem does not lie in the choice of material or of methods. It lies in the secular orientation of American Protestants who find that they can live effectively without the Bible. Until or unless they find otherwise, they will continue to espouse its use—for children.

VI. Other Fields of Discussion

This discussion has outlined developments in the United States. A similar account could be given of Canada; both the United Church of Canada and the Anglicans are using experience-oriented curricula. In England, the agreed syllabi which formed the bases for religious learning in the school were strongly biblical. These have been under attack by Ronald Goldman, Principal of Didsbury College of Education, Manchester, whose research has indicated that they seem to produce more confusion than light. His co-workers are developing experience-centred courses of study.

The discussion could have been paralleled by references to recent developments in American Catholic curricula, most of which are now biblically oriented within the framework of a liturgical and sacramental understanding. The Bible is apparent as holy history in the *Come to the Father series* (Paulist Press), an import from Canada, and in *The Christian Inheritance* series, a Christian Brothers' publication. The life-experience approach is more effectively presented in several Catholic curricula than in any Protestant series. Such Catholic series include *Time for Living* (Herder and Herder), *Life, Love, Joy,* developed by the National Center of the Confraternity of Christian Doctrine (Silver Burdett, publishers), and Argus Communications' multi-media presentations for youth and adults. Protestant parishes are among their most eager users.

The Bible comes to us as the written record of the word of God, and—for people who like to read—this is a useful form of communication. The McLuhan thesis of a new tribalism should make us reflect that the Bible began as an oral tradition. The story needs to be heard: to be told by person to person, to be witnessed to in personal and community experience, and to be celebrated in the liturgy. The next attempts at curriculum re-writing may have to take seriously such kinds of response to the Bible.

CURRICULAR MATERIALS NOTED

Choose Life (Argus Communications, Chicago, 1968 ff.).

Christian Faith and Action (Board of Christian Education, United Presbyterian Church, Philadelphia, 1970).

Christian Faith and Work Plan (American Baptist Convention, Judson Graded Series, Valley Forge, 1969).

The Christian Inheritance (St Mary's College Press, Winona, Minn.; a Christian Brothers' publication, distributed by Liturgical Press, Collegeville, 1968 ff.).

The Church's Teaching Series (Seabury Press, NYC, 1955 ff.).

Come to the Father (Paulist Press, Glen Rock, NJ, 1966 ff.).

Covenant Life Curriculum (Covenant Life Press, Richmond, 1964 ff.).

Sunday Church School Series (Lutheran Church of America, Lutheran Church Press, Philadelphia, 1964 ff.).

Time for Living (Herder and Herder, NYC, 1968 ff.).

United Church Curriculum (United Church Press, Philadelphia, 1962 ff.).

Wesley Series (United Methodist Church, the Graded Press, Nashville, 1967 ff.).

Onésimo O'Gorman

"Renewed" Catechisms in South America

I. THE CATECHETICAL MOVEMENT IN GENERAL

SOUTH AMERICA is only a part of Latin America, since it excludes the Antilles, Central America and Mexico. Portuguese is spoken in Brazil and Spanish in the remaining countries. The continent is free from racial problems. Leaving out the enclave of the Guyanas, it is made up of ten independent republics: from North to South—Venezuela, Colombia, Ecuador, Brazil, Peru, Bolivia, Paraguay, Uruguay, Chile and Argentina.

The evangelization of the continent was originally carried out by Spanish and Portuguese missionaries; the religious orders from these two countries bore the brunt of the work, and were aided by priests and religious of other nationalities.

1. *The Present Situation*

The catechetical movement is active at present because pastors and the Christian community as a whole realized that the religious convictions and ways of life in these countries were in a precarious state. The Sixth International Week of Catechesis was held at Medellín in Colombia, in August 1968. Its purpose was to examine the problems of pastoral catechesis throughout the continent. Popular religious expression was taken as the point of reference for the elaboration of a pastoral theology of evangelization and catechesis for Latin America. The discussions were full of interest and the plans made full of promise for a better future in this aspect of the Church's work. The occasion was the beginning of an era of greater enthusiasm and better co-ordination in studies on regional, national and continental levels, designed to promote more effective action.

Pastoral circles are more and more concerned that catechesis should get away from the quantitative criterion ("to reach the greatest possible number of people") to the qualitative dimension ("to reach people in the best possible way"). This has resulted in the intensified production of new and updated material, as well as in an intensified drive to educate good catechists. So there has been a large increase in the numbers of schools, seminaries and catechetical institutes on all levels, in the conviction that efficient catechists are needed if catechetical methods and resources are to be put to effective use.

"Formation through action" is the norm everywhere. To put this into effect, "teacher's guides" to accompany the catechetical manuals were asked for—and provided practically everywhere. These give guidelines to the catechists in planning their work, enabling them to interpret their material better and teaching them a more spontaneous approach, better suited to their surroundings.

2. Stages of Catechetical Development

A few prefatory remarks are necessary before going on to review the "renewed" catechisms that have had most influence. Not long ago the abbreviated catechisms by Frs Astete and Ripalda were in almost exclusive use, with a few amplified or adapted versions such as the Catechism of Santo Toribio for Peru, that by Mgr Arias in Venezuela and the one produced by the bishops of the Argentine, which was also used in Uruguay and Bolivia. A few other versions, identical in content and methodology, were produced in different countries.

The next stage was the introduction of foreign manuals and series, with adaptations of varying extent and validity. This was undoubtedly a useful experiment, and filled an urgent need. Some of these works are still in use.

Now each country is making an effort to produce material adequately adapted to the needs of its people, which means that the number of new books is large, and that it is difficult to trace them all and evaluate their influence. A great deal of material is now being produced on the results of surveys of the anthropological, socio-cultural and psycho-religious conditions of the faithful; this promises soon to have a considerable influence on the pastoral effort.

The readership of each book is being considerably refined. The "national catechism" or "sole text" is giving way to a varied selection of books planned in different series, for children, adolescents and adults, and for parishes, schools and colleges; there are special works for use by specialized groups such as university students, workers, farm labourers, and so on. This means that each particular work has a more restricted application. So the best way to give an overall view seems to be to take each country separately, in alphabetical order, despite the inevitable limitations of this method.

II. The Efforts of Different Countries

1. *Argentina*

A catechism that opened new horizons in Argentinian catechesis and spread to other countries in Latin America was *Iniciación en la Vida Cristiana* (Initiation into Christian Life), with its accompanying teacher's guide, prepared by Fr Juan C. Ruta and a team of catechists. Its basic aim was to help children in their first steps in the Christian life by gradually unveiling the mystery of Christ to them, through a series of images carefully adapted to children's minds. This is a biblical catechesis in that it starts from the word of God as the prime source of knowledge of the major themes of salvation history. The unifying theme of the book is the paschal mystery in its different stages. This makes it a liturgical catechesis as well. The doctrinal content follows naturally from the word of God and the liturgy. The final synthesis aimed at is the mystery of the Church as continuing the threefold mission of Christ. The book is divided into lessons, and the outline generally follows the structure of the celebration of the Word, the teacher's guide being a powerful help to its use.

This book is used particularly in preparation for the sacraments of penance and the Eucharist; but its authors did not stop there, and complemented it with a further volume entitled *Mi Confirmación*, a textbook with teacher's guide following the same lines as their previous book. The instruction here is directed towards forging an ecclesial consciousness, particularly a sense of belonging to the diocesan community and the parish community within that.

Another catechetical work that has been widely distributed and had considerable influence is *Para ser felices con Jesus* (To be happy with Jesus), which likewise has a teacher's guide. It was originally published in one loose-leaf volume, then, when several dioceses laid down two years as the minimum period of preparation for penance and the Eucharist, it was divided into two volumes, with some extra material added to each. The loose-leaf work sheets are designed to involve parents in the religious education of their children.

The plan starts from the idea of happiness and examines it from various angles to give an existential setting to Christian initiation, with the whole Christian message presented within the framework of the history of salvation. Particular emphasis is placed on baptism, as a rebirth to the life of God in the Christian family, and the prime mediator of happiness. The sacraments, commandments and prayers are introduced throughout the book as their respective doctrinal themes emerge from the Bible. The book was produced by a team of qualified catechists under the general editorship of Mgr Alberto Devoto and Fr Alfredo B. Trusso. It went into several editions and is still in use. It was published by Editorial Bonum, in Buenos Aires.

Fr Ismael Calcagno and Sr Gabriela Etchebarne have produced a catechetical series for Christian initiation; its reputation is justifiably high in catechetical circles throughout the country. The following volumes have already been published: *Dios nos llama* (God calls Us), a book for the catechist for the first year of initiation, giving a lesson scheme; *Aquí estoy, Señor* (Here I am, Lord), the corresponding children's book; *Introducción a la Vida comunitaria* (Introduction to Community Life), folders with celebrations corresponding to the lesson themes of the previous books, expressing the signs presented in them in the shape of liturgical activity; *Cantemos al Señor* (Let's sing to the Lord), a pamphlet with songs and acclamations to be used in the catechetical lessons. The catechist's book for the second year is *Que te conozcan, Señor* (That they may know you, Lord), containing the scheme of the lessons and their corresponding celebrations, with an Appendix on preparation for penance and outlines of children's Masses; the children's book is called *Dáme tu Pan, Señor* (Give me your Bread, Lord), and there is a very useful adjunct of ten visual aids specially prepared for the series, and three records of psalms and liturgical songs. The same authors are preparing further volumes in the series, and also a catechesis for kindergarten children and a pamphlet for mothers' centres.

The authors describe the plan of their work like this: "The historical and progressive unfolding of the plan of salvation appears as a backdrop throughout this programme, from the creation of the universe to the second coming of Jesus and the definitive union of all the redeemed with the triune God. But we would stress that this historical outline is not the real plan. Our constant preoccupation has been to put the child in direct contact with Christ. The historical facts are 'signs' whose purpose is to facilitate the encounter between the individual and the Word of God 'incarnate': Christ, our Covenant. Through his consideration of the historical events, the child should penetrate ever more deeply into the mystery of God who became *one of us*."

The method is conceived on the basis of biblical, liturgical and testimonial signs with the intention of arriving at an assimilation of their deeper meaning. Sacramental catechesis makes frequent use of symbols as the most effective way of inculcating religious experience.

Sr Gabriela Etchebarne's team has also produced a catechetical series for handicapped children that has been particularly successful. The following books have been published for the use of catechists handling special groups: *Alleluia, para tí, Señor* (Alleluia for you, Lord), for mentally retarded children, and *Resuscitaremos, Alleluia* (We shall rise again, Alleluia), for sick and physically handicapped children.

Ediciones Búsqueda, directed by Fr Juan J. Rossi, is publishing a graded series of textbooks for parishes and colleges, of which three have so far appeared, each with its respective teacher's guide: *El Señor viene* (The Lord is coming), *Jesús es nuestro amigo* (Jesus is our Friend) and *Somos tesitos de Jesús* (We are Jesus' Witnesses). These are a systematic attempt to initiate children into the Christian faith progressively, using the psychological approach suited to their age. This consists of education in the meaning of God, the encounter with Jesus, the child's attitudes to life and his participation in the sacraments of the Eucharist, penance and confirmation, as well as an appreciation of the meaning of his baptism.

The method used is *progressive* in its development of content, and *active* in the way its catechesis is carried forward through meetings. Parents are required to participate in the religious education of their children. The first stage of this systematized catechesis situates the child in the universe of revelation and creation, and brings him to realize the presence of the divine persons, through an analogy with the little world of his own personal relations—parents, friends, brothers and sisters, and so on.

The textbook gives the catechist four well-defined elements for each lesson: (a) didactic notes, whose aim is to give the basic meaning of the lesson and present the solutions to the problems as well as the elements to be borne in mind for the preparation and development of the theme; (b) the outline of each lesson, which gives concrete suggestions for the presentation of each theme to the children; (c) notes on activities, with a brief explanation of the activity corresponding to each lesson; (d) notes on the illustrations and the means of using them in each meeting; each textbook is profusely illustrated in colour.

The Daughters of St Paul have also started a series, of which the following titles have been published: *Padre Nuestro* (Our Father), *Jesús, soy tu testigo* (Jesus, I am your Witness), *Jesus, yo creo en tí* (Jesus, I believe in you), *El Señor viene* (The Lord is coming), *Vivimos la pascua* (We live Easter), and *Héroes del pueblo de Dios* (Heroes of the People of God), each with its respective teacher's guide. The work is aimed at fulfilling the requirements of the catechetical renewal through an appreciation of the Bible and the liturgy, with a christocentric approach and adaptation of the message to the children's mentality. The guides also contain elements designed to further the spiritual and catechetical formation of their users. Also published by Ediciones Paulinas in the Argentine is the series *Imitadores de Cristo* (Imitators of Christ) by Prof. Andrés Dossin, for secondary schools, of which five titles have been published, plus teacher's guides. These have been reprinted in their country of origin, and there have been editions made in Chile and Colombia, with slight adaptations, as well as a translation into Portuguese for Brazil.

The plan of this work follows the requirements of the bishops of the Argentine for secondary schools, and each lesson follows the same pattern: biblical text, establishment of the basic idea, analysis of the text, doctrinal synthesis, basic elements, applications to life.

2. *Bolivia*

The nascent catechetical movement of this land of the Andes, with its mainly native and *mestizo* population, is the work of the National Catechetical Office. In 1964 its members, to get away from the catechism of question and answer, began publishing a transitional series that has had a profound influence. This collection, *Agua de vida* (Water of Life), was designed for schools and parishes and consists of six volumes, each with a teacher's guide. *Padre nuestro* initiates the child into the Christian life, and starts from gestures and attitudes familiar to him from his surroundings; it has very little text and a few schematic drawings; *Soy hijo del Padre* (I am the Father's Child) refers particularly to baptism and the person of Christ as shown in the gospels; *Soy Iglesia: el Señor me ha llamado* (I am the Church: the Lord has called me) goes from the Old Testament to the encounter with Christ, particularly through the sacraments of penance and the Eucharist; *Sigo los pasos del Maestro* (I follow the Master's Footsteps) emphasizes the meaning of the response to God's call through Christ—the Christian life; *El Señor está cerca* (The Lord is near) is a more specific invitation to faith through more direct contact with the Gospel. There is another series for the basic secondary education course, three volumes following the progressive outline of the history of salvation, entitled *El Salvador, Los signos del Señor* and *El Maestro* (The Saviour, The Signs of the Lord, and The Master). The whole collection was produced under a team directed by Fr José Prats and Sr Teresita Jackel.

3. *Brazil*

The great extent and variety of population of this huge country make a catechetical bibliography difficult to compile. It is possible to mention here only a few of the many textbooks that exist. The training of catechists and the production of textbooks are handled by Higher Institutes of Pastoral Catechetics (ISPAC). The works published are tied in with overall regional pastoral plans, co-ordinated at national level for use in each diocese.

The ISPAC of Rio de Janeiro has published an interesting text-book for the very poor, called *A Boa Nova e anunciada aos Pobres* (The Good News is announced to the Poor), edited by Sr Agostinho Roy. It is a work of catechesis and evangelization, designed to promote human dignity—a factor common to all Brazilian pastoral work—and centred upon the ideas of friendship and God's covenant with men, among whom he specially seeks out the poor, in order to dignify them as human beings created in his "image and likeness". Each catechetical meeting is organized around the theme of the word: the word meditated on, the word proclaimed, the word accepted, the word kept, the word put into action.

Another interesting work from the same centre is *Planos para uma Catequese de Adolescentes* (Outlines for an Adolescent Cate-chesis), prepared by a committee under the general direction of Sr Sylvia Villac, who is responsible for the centre's experiments in the religious education of girls. The collection includes guides for schoolchildren and youth groups. Its theme centres on the personal encounter with Christ which stems from "the deep aspirations, wishes and desires and the intimate problems of young people". Each session opens with the search for an "atti-tude of mind" in those taking part, which is considered in full session and then studied more deeply in teams in the light of the Gospel. Several pamphlets have been published, with titles such as "My New Encounter with Christ", "Christ is calling me to build my Personality". A similar work has been prepared in Bahía, for the North-East of Brazil. It is called *Descuberta de un Tesouro* and is designed specially for the particular conditions of that part of the country.

In the South, the team of the "Juventude" Cultural Centre in Porto Alegre has produced a series of catechetical manuals for adolescents, together with teacher's guides and outlines for group leaders. They have titles like "The Master calls you!", "Live!", "Grow!", "Take up your Bed!", and try to go direct to the main interests of young people in order to make them reflect on their relationship to present-day society, and their relationship to God as Christians. Once the theme and aim of each meeting have been fixed, a basis for the aim in everyday life is found, and the obstacles that stand in the way of its fulfilment are examined; work-groups then try to find a Christian meaning in this aspect of everyday life through meditating on the word of God; different types of activity are included in each meeting.

Crescemos Construindo (We grow up building) and *Escola Secundaria e Fe cristiana* (Secondary School and Christian Faith) are two revised textbooks by Fr Claudio Ortiga. They start from the life and concerns of young people today so as to lead them to reflect on their task in the world and to a knowledge of the Lord of history. Each work session is designed to last two hours, starting with an introduction to the subject, followed by work in groups, then a general discussion and a written summary directed towards immediate action to be taken, and the assignment of individual activities.

A team of the Sisters of Jesus Crucified has produced a collection of textbooks for catechesis in schools and parishes on the following themes: "Your Encounter with Jesus", "I want to follow Jesus", "With Jesus we find Peace", "Peace, that we may all be One", "We walk towards the Light". Their effectiveness has been proved over several years, and they are continually revised and brought up to date.

4. *Colombia*

The catechetical renewal in this country has started from a re-working of the catechetical syllabuses for schools, now that religious instruction in the schools is once more allowed. The new schemes, each designed to last a year, mark a transitional stage. Each subject is divided into the message to put across, objectives to be realized, statements to remember, biblical and liturgical texts, and appropriate prayers. There are several series of text-books and teacher's guides, and each diocese is free to choose its own. One series is written by Mgr José Gabriel Calderón, the president of the Episcopal Catechetical Commission, and is widely used. Its fifth-year book is divided into separate pamphlets, appropriately illustrated. Another widely used series is published by Ediciones Paulinas, prepared by a team which has also produced separate books for preparation for communion and penance, and there is a third series on similar lines entitled *Luz y Vida* (Light and Life).

5. *Chile*

Chile has produced a different type of catechetical material, in the shape of a "Basic Catechism of the Chilean Episcopate". The Episcopal Catechetical Commission entrusted a group of theologians and pastors with the task of producing a catechism, in question and answer form, to serve as a guide for all works of evangelization and catechesis to be published for different environments, age groups and levels of Christian life. It is not designed to induce rigid conformity, but to introduce a uniformity in formulating the Christian message. The formulas are not necessarily to be learnt by heart. The group was directed by Joaquín Matte Varas and Florencio Hofmans, and after lengthy study and consultation with experts in various disciplines, presented the project, which was officially promulgated by the Episcopal Catechetical Commission on 18 April 1965.

The introduction to the book—which contains four parts with a total of 341 questions and answers, each preceded by one, two or three asterisks to indicate the specific level—sets out the content and indicates the way it should be used. Its basic ideas are summed up like this: the love of God, our Father, who calls us to his kingdom; God's mercy incarnate in Christ; Christ dead and risen presides over the ecclesial community: he is our life; in the liturgy and the sacraments we meet Christ and the Church; living according to the commandments is an expression of our love of God: our imitation of Christ; summing everything up in a lived charity is the soul of the whole Christian life; the meaning of our life is that now we live in a "prefiguration" of the fullness to come: we wait and long for the manifestation of the Lord.

This basic content is prepared solely for catechetical writers, who can use it in accordance with different pedagogical methods and at different levels of learning, to suit their particular audiences. It is up to them to illustrate the themes with biblical and liturgical texts, prayers, and so on. Of various other valuable works published in different towns in Chile both before and after this basic catechism, I would mention *Es el Señor* (It is the Lord), for mothers who help to prepare their children for the sacraments of initiation.

6. *Ecuador*

In 1967 the National Catechetical Commission of the Episcopal Conference of Ecuador published the "Popular Catechism", subtitled "The Message of Christian Life". The introduction sets out its basic theme and methodology: "The book's inner structure presents religion as a historic-salvific event. Its object is to show God's way of saving man as faithfully as possible. God's intervention in history and man's response, throughout the history of salvation, is an attractive and fascinating fact. Each lesson follows a method that might be called kerygmatic: announcement of the message, explanation, doctrinal synthesis and reply." The work represents a valuable step forward along the road of post-conciliar renewal. As in Chile, various textbooks and teacher's guides are now being prepared along the lines it lays down, more particularly adapted to their audiences.

7. *Paraguay*

Fr Osvaldo Aveiro Stark has recently published a manual for catechists and parents preparing their children for the sacraments of penance and the Eucharist, called *Encuentros personales con Dios: viviendo su palabra* (Personal Encounters with God: living his Word). It is a clear and very practical account of the message, biblical and liturgical in orientation, with an emphasis on making faith live in the catechumen through a personal encounter with God, through his word. Methodologically each subject starts with a discussion on everyday life which leads to the encounter of prayer and the sacraments. It is a work that will clearly have considerable influence in catechetical circles in Paraguay.

8. *Peru*

In Peru, with its great geographical and ethnic variety, various pastoral experiments are in hand. Two catechetical centres are producing new material: one in Cuzco, directed by Fr Juan de Dios and Fr Joaquín Meseger, writing both for schoolchildren and native adults, and another in the National Catechetical Office in Lima, headed by Fr Santiago Izuzquiza and a team of specialists.

The books currently in use are based loosely on the Canadian "Come to the Father" series, which has been taken as a basis in the task of providing a renewed catechesis. The series is used in the archdiocese of Lima, and in such diverse areas as Pucallpa, Paramonga, Huacho, Chincha, Ica and Chiclayo. Its content is resolutely biblical and liturgical and it makes use of Peruvian folk elements—dances, songs and games—in its method.

9. *Uruguay*

The principal centres producing catechetical material in Uruguay are those of Montevideo and San José de Mayo. The Archdiocesan Catechetical Office of Montevideo has produced a series for Christian initiation in three volumes; it is also used in other dioceses in the interior. Each volume has a teacher's guide, a notebook for meetings with parents, and weekly work cards for them. Each of the three stages culminates with one of the three sacraments of initiation: penance, Eucharist, confirmation. Meetings with the parents to encourage them to take part in the Christian initiation of their children are envisaged before the catechists meet the children. Each lesson starts from a basic human experience: family, locality, school, and so on. Apart from this series, a work-group of religious sisters and lay people directed by Fr Roberto Viola has produced a very effective series of pamphlets for the evangelization and catechesis of adults.

10. *Venezuela*

The dawning movement of catechetical renewal in this country is apparent in several new schemes for schools, parishes and catechetical centres. Meanwhile, the Archdiocesan Catechetical Centre of Caracas has published a syllabus of lesson plans prepared by a team of sisters of the order of Our Lady of Lourdes, directed by Fr Enrique Llorente. These plans, covering all the primary school years, are accompanied by teacher's guides and have served as the point of departure for all the new books now in preparation. Complementary material available includes a series of work cards for each form and a book of preparation for first communion by Pedro Huysman and Cornelio Voordeckers.

Translated by Paul Burns

Luigi Della Torre

Reflections on the Isolotto Catechism

AT A TIME when events in the parish of Isolotto had aroused keen public interest,[1] an announcement by the Archbishop of Florence drew attention to the so-called *Isolotto Catechism*. It concluded, "On examination, the contents do not conform to the acceptable standards of an orthodox catechism and therefore the Cardinal Archbishop, with deep regret, forbids its use in this Arch-diocese."[2] The catechism, which has two parts—one a catechists' guide, the other a series of recommendations for running chil-dren's study groups—received no more than an *ad instar manu-scripti*.[3]

The full effects of this pastoral pronouncement on the practice of religion in the parish of Isolotto cannot be calculated immedi-ately; time alone will tell what the full results will be.[4]

The following remarks are therefore limited to an examination of the aims and day-to-day practice of the scheme.

[1] Cf. *Informations catholiques internationales*, n. 324, 1968, 11. For fuller information, see *Isolotto 1954–1969* (Laterza, Bari, 1969).

[2] *Op. cit.*, p. 243.

[3] The Parish of Isolotto, *Incontro a Gesù, Guida per la iniziazione dei ragazzi al mistero di Cristo*, p. 86 (L.E.F., Florence, 1968), with nineteen schemes, in folder. German edition (Grünewald-Kaiser, Mainz-Munich, 1969), with an introduction by A. Exeler. French edition in preparation (Ed. du Cerf).

[4] This assumes that the community at Isolotto will be able to continue its unique experiment in religious instruction. The present account was written in July 1969. The ecclesiastical ruling, by using a restrictive tradi-tional formula, does not seem to appreciate the real nature of the scheme, or seem concerned with its positive development.

I. An Introduction to the Christian Way of Life with Reference to an Actual Community

Consideration of *Incontro a Gesù* as a catechism has led too many to make hasty and unjust judgments. Nowhere in the text is there any attempt to define it as such, nor does it claim to be a definitive and comprehensive exposition of Christian doctrine, fully adapted to all the needs of children. It was designed as a practical working document to be used as a guide by catechists when introducing children of ten and over to the living mystery of Christ and the daily practice of the Christian life. The compilers of the guide say, "As we come to understand more fully the practical obligations of Christianity in the daily life of a community, we find that the methods we recommend for bringing our children to a closer union with Christ must be subjected to constant review."[5]

The project began in 1954 on a new housing estate built for 3,000 people (immigrants from the South, or from rural areas, skilled and unskilled workers from the most crowded areas of Florence collected in this new district).[6] Don Enzo Mazzi was appointed to be their parish priest. In 1957 a group of several priests and about a hundred laypeople was formed. It was characterized "by a strong community spirit and it deliberately tried not to define its aims too precisely, nor to limit its membership too strictly, since it wanted to remain open to everyone". Its principal aim was to study the Bible and to draw inspiration and instruction from it for the creation of a fuller personal and socially responsible life. As part of the housing estate, they were in a unique position to understand and to help solve specific problems of the community (unemployment, lack of essential social services, and so on); in an effort to create a community based on true Christian principles, they tried to become as closely integrated as possible with the area.[7] The moral force and social strength of this community were demonstrated by the efforts made to obtain firm guarantees of work for the unemployed, by protests to obtain better school conditions, and by requests for aid

[5] *Incontro a Gesù*, p. 7.
[6] There are at present 13,000 people in the district.
[7] *Isolotto 1954–1969*, p. 17.

to victims of the destructive flood that swept through Florence. In spite of this, the scheme met with the disapproval of the local ecclesiastical authorities, who were frightened of being made the dupes of extremist political organizations.

The new atmosphere created by the Ecumenical Council gave the group confirmation of the value of their scheme and encouragement to continue to identify themselves with the "Church of the poor". They showed the genuineness of their Christian faith by a sympathetic identification with the underprivileged and oppressed. So they were led to examine the need for peace in Vietnam, the problems of the coloured people in the United States and of people in the underdeveloped countries of Latin America, the need for freedom in Czechoslovakia; to understand sympathetically the problems of human misfits in society; to press for aid to those who had lost their homes during the earthquakes in Sicily; and to uphold the rights of conscientious objectors. They saw this programme not only as an exercise of social conscience, but as a positive demonstration of Christian principles derived from a genuine commitment to the teaching of the gospels.[8]

The community at Isolotto tried to bring its children into contact with this vital, practical exercise of the Christian religion.

II. The Methodology and Aims of this Initiation into the "Mystery of Christ": Practical Working Method

When they are about ten years old, the children are first brought into contact with the practical examination of religious values during instruction for their first holy communion. In groups of two or three, they are instructed for about seven months by a mature person who, together with them, tries to follow the Christian way of life. These instructors or catechists can be workers or students or mothers of families. There were forty of them in 1963, sixty in 1964; and they continued their work in 1969 in spite of the official suspension of all pastoral activities. "They are united by the firmest bonds of friendship; have gained a wider knowledge through their work; understand Christ's

[8] An attempt to relate Christian teaching to the life and events of today can be seen in *Isolotto 1954–1969*, pp. 70–90.

teaching more fully and can appreciate the value of a genuinely Christian community. Yet they know how much more there remains for them to learn. . . . The instructor, together with the children, creates a small Christian family which tries to lead its daily life in accordance with the values to be found in the gospels."[9]

Each group is offered a programme of study and any other help it may need. The programme itself is no more than a working method for group study, and does not in any way offer opinions on doctrinal matters. It has three main divisions: the study of mankind; the study of Christ's teaching; and the practice of religious values in one's own life. The first part deals with life, defined as "either everyday life or as the story of human life seen throughout history". In this study, human life is seen to derive its true value from the teaching of Christ, a fact which is continually stressed. "Then the group begins to study a particular event in the Gospel and moves from there to a study of the whole body of religious teaching contained in it." This second stage is considered to be "the most important part of the scheme". After that, great care must be taken when the group moves from the study of the religious teaching of the Gospel to its relevance in one's daily life. At this stage one must at all costs avoid the temptation of "using Christ's teaching to justify and reinforce the particular moral code of any one culture or social class".[10] During the twenty-five meetings suggested in the scheme, the children are encouraged to make a vital and personal acquaintance with Christ's teaching and to realize that he invites them to close bonds of friendship and to a fuller understanding of his Father, of his mother and of the circumstances of his birth, and upbringing. From there, study is directed towards those aspects of Jesus' life where he is seen as teacher and saviour, then to the events leading up to his death, and finally to a realization of the significance of the resurrection and of his continuing presence and influence in the Church and in the world.

III. UNDERLYING PRINCIPLES

The scheme and its application are strongly influenced by

[9] *Incontro a Gesù*, p. 13.   [10] *Op. cit.*, p. 15.

certain religious convictions which are characteristic of the community of Isolotto. They are summarized as follows in the guide given for the use of instructors:[11]

1. Christ's influence extends through the history of mankind and permeates human experience.

2. In Christ, all purposeful human and social activity towards a better world finds true fulfilment.

3. In every century and particularly in the present one, the restorative power of Christ's message is to be applied to human sufferings, to man's aspirations and their fulfilment, and to all moral and social struggles which have their origins in the poorest and most rejected of mankind.

4. Human life has full meaning only when it is centred on Christ, and particularly when it is directed towards the discovery of truth and the knowledge of God.

IV. The Study of the Significance of Human Life is open to all

When the group begins to study the meaning of "life" it limits itself neither to personal experiences, nor to a situation chosen carefully for its suitability as an example of moral instruction. It is prepared to deal with any social or historical event relevant to its aims. Later on, discussion extends to the children's own family and environment and then to those countries where the poor and oppressed struggle for liberty and security of life. In the scheme of work, accompanying photographs help to illustrate the points for discussion. Instructors are given clear guiding lines to use in stimulating and directing group study, especially "in difficult though important discussions", as for example, pointing out (when dealing with Christ's own youth) the differences between the upbringing and attitudes of the son of a rich family and those of a poor one. Yet, "no attempt is made to establish or maintain any prejudice in the minds of the children; every effort is made to make them appreciate the realities of the social situation; for only by such impartial and realistic examination can they be helped to overcome their already existing prejudices. To attempt to hide reality on the grounds that it is too harsh can

[11] Op. cit., pp. 8–12.

only help those in whose interests it is to create and maintain such prejudices."[12] At this point in the scheme, when the group is studying the history of mankind, reference is made to specific events in the story of the Jewish race, seen as an example of an oppressed people assisted by God towards their true destiny.

V. Christ and the Practice of the Christian Way of Life

Instructors are advised not to assume that the gospels provide exact instructions, perfectly adapted to the Christian way of life, "or it will be assumed that the gospels exist merely to justify a doctrinaire concept of life".[13] In the study of the gospels, particular attention is paid to Christ's words and actions in the context of the religious and social conditions of his time. Special emphasis is laid on: the poverty of Christ's family; his message to the underprivileged, the poor and sinful, to whom he gave help and assurances of freedom and salvation; the fact that his teaching fulfils God's promise to Abraham and indicates that essential wholeness of being towards which he, as saviour and good shepherd, is leading all mankind; the power of love of which he is the greatest exemplar; the reality of the opposition to his teaching by the arrogance and hatred of those powerful forces which opposed and finally killed him; the significance of the Last Supper both as a memorial and living source of Christian love; the resurrection, seen as a historical truth from which many important principles are to be derived; the victory of Christian love over self-centredness, of liberty over tyranny, and of life over death.

Similar emphases are to be found in the scheme given to the various study groups to help them realize Christ's presence in, and the applicability of his teaching to everyday life. The scheme aims to demonstrate the eschatological framework of history, and to do this in a realistic and non-doctrinaire way. The following examples will illustrate the procedure: to find out whether it is true that even today the salvation of the world depends on the meek and poor in spirit; to help the children understand that Christ does not really recommend that the poor should resign themselves to suffering and hunger in this world as a necessary

[12] *Op. cit.*, p. 38.   [13] *Op. cit.*, p. 15.

prerequisite for bliss in the next; to emphasize the reality of Christ's union with those who at present struggle to help man free himself from evils and oppression; to realize the significance of the gradual progression of humanity towards the Christian concepts of love, justice, brotherhood and peace; to illustrate the genuine resemblance of the lives and principles of some people to Christ's own; to demonstrate the fullness of love shown by Christ and its frightening absence in many of those professing Christianity.

The last three meetings are devoted to the study of the living presence of Christ in the practice of the Church's liturgy. Here real difficulties are created by the fact that both Church liturgy and ecclesiastical life are profoundly dissociated from daily life. "The instructors engage in mental gymnastics in trying to make certain aspects of the liturgy comprehensible, when surely its original intention was to stimulate not deaden response. Their attempts to do so sometimes make them look ridiculous, at other times intellectually dishonest." In the face of this instructors are advised "to tell the children of fresh ideas and new methods of revitalizing the Church's liturgy which are now being used".[14]

VI. The Advantages and Disadvantages of the Scheme

The limitations of *Incontro a Gesù* are well understood by its compilers. Such limitations were further underlined by the pronouncement from the Archbishop of Florence.[15] Yet they do not maintain that their scheme represents "a fully comprehensive exposition of Christ's teaching to boys of ten years of age and over", nor do they assume that it is final and definitive: "This wide-ranging introduction should prepare the way for fuller and deeper

---

[14] *Op. cit.*, p. 74.

[15] "It is possible that the contents of a text meant for children should be simplified, but it must contain all essential religious teaching" (*Isolotto 1954-1969*, p. 242). It is surprising that the pronouncement claims that, in the scheme, "the essential teachings of the Christian Religion have been omitted"; here the "essential teaching" is identified with the resurrection. In fact all twenty-three meetings are dedicated to this theme, and an awareness of the risen Christ's abiding presence in the world and in the Church influences the whole scheme. The effect that this pronouncement is having on the lives of the faithful will be readily appreciated.

study of Biblical and doctrinal teaching."[16] Actual participation in the Church's liturgy and periodic reunions of every study group in a paraliturgical context should ensure the fuller integration and development of the programme initiated by the instructors.

It should be observed that during the development of the scheme from an earlier phase (about which there is a wealth of documentation) to the present one, a decision was taken—not without careful thought—to abandon both the more rigidly dogmatic teaching given by the clergy in recent months and the formal prayer sessions after the reading of the gospels. An agreement was reached in 1963 to include doctrinal teaching in the scheme, especially that concerning the sacraments and the Mass. But by 1966 it was agreed that no real solution had been found as how best to teach these aspects of religion and that it was "necessary to make further efforts to discover a method and language more suitable for genuine communication".[17] With regard to the formal prayers, it must be recognized that their over-formality leads to rejection by the children and that one should look upon every meeting as a form of prayer, especially those for the reading of the gospels, in a group or in individual study. The instructors do not assume that they have solved all problems and always try to base their actions on careful thought.

The fundamental advantage and, in certain contexts, immense value of this scheme is that it attempts to show children the efforts of a real community to lead a life based on Christian principles. Great care is taken to avoid the mechanical teaching of religious formulae which are seen to have nothing to do with their daily lives. A child who experiences, however incompletely, that the religious instruction he receives has actual relevance to his daily life can more easily understand the significance of other, perhaps more difficult, aspects of the Catholic faith. Another advantage, derived from the social and cultural attitudes of the community, is the attempt made to free religion from its over-conceptualized and abstract connotations, so that God's word to man becomes a living message giving hope and meaning to the whole of our daily lives.

[16] *Incontro a Gesù*, p. 14.   [17] *Isolotto 1954–1969*, p. 99.

Translated by P. McCourt